A Cottage Herbal

A Cottage Herbal

Elizabeth Cullum

DAVID & CHARLES

Newton Abbot   London

North Pomfret (VT)   Vancouver

For

Sally and Timothy

ISBN 0 7153 7108 8
Library of Congress Catalog Card Number 75 10563

© ELIZABETH CULLUM 1975

Set in 11 on 13pt Plantin
and printed in Great Britain
by Latimer Trend & Company Ltd Plymouth
for David & Charles (Holdings) Limited
South Devon House Newton Abbot Devon

Published in the United States of America
by David & Charles Inc
North Pomfret Vermont 05053 USA

Published in Canada
by Douglas David & Charles Limited
132 Philip Avenue North Vancouver BC

Contents

Illustrations

Plates

The above plates are reproduced from photographs by
Keith E. Cullum

Author's Note

Botanically a herb is a plant that is not woody but dies back to a rootstock in winter, thus excluding many shrubs and plants such as thyme and rosemary. For the purpose of this book I have taken the old meaning of the word herb as any plant that is useful or beneficial to man. Nearly all the plants in the book grow in my garden or in the lanes and meadows around my cottage, and it is from these plants that I have taken the drawings.

Elizabethan Herb Song

Plant me a garden to heal the body,
Betony, yarrow and daisies to mend,
Sage for the blood and comfrey for bones
Foxglove and hyssop the sick to tend.

Tansy, rosemary, rue and thyme,
Bring back the lover who once was mine,
I will give him the sweet Basil tree
Then he will always belong to me.

Plant me a garden to heal the heart,
Balm for joy, and the sweet violet
Cowslips, pansies and chamomile
To ease the pain I want to forget.

Tansy, rosemary, rue and thyme,
Bring back the lover who once was mine,
I will give him the sweet Basil tree
Then he will always belong to me.

Plant me a garden to heal the soul,
A garden of peace and tranquillity,
Soothed with the scent of lavender
And the heavenly blue of chicory.

Tansy, rosemary, rue and thyme,
Bring back the lover who once was mine,
I will give him the sweet Basil tree
Then he will always belong to me.

Introduction

When we bought a Tudor cottage in a country hamlet surrounded by cornfields we became fascinated by its history. It was a fairy-tale cottage, the thick thatched roof sheltering it against the winter storms and dipping down to the little latticed windows and green painted door. A feeling of peace and tranquillity that seemed to belong to a past age surrounded the house and grounds. In summer the garden was warm and peaceful, full of birdsong and the humming of bees. Stepping into it was like stepping back in time and I longed to know more about all the people who had lived here before us and grown to love the 400-year-old cottage as I did.

In reading about the way people lived centuries ago I realised how much they depended on plants, not only for food, but for many other purposes. Their clothes were dyed with leaves, bark and berries. They made brushes with broom and hazel twigs, baskets from hedgerow shrubs and candles by soaking rushes and mullein stalks in animal fat. There was no medicine as we know it now. People had to depend on what were known as 'simples' – mixtures prepared from herbs and plants. Many of the so-called cures must have been merely good fortune, although some of our drugs today are derived from plants and used to treat the same illnesses as they were in medieval times. The best known of these are digitalis from foxgloves and the drugs atropine and hyoscyamine from deadly nightshade (belladonna).

During my searches I came across a copy of Culpeper's *Complete Herbal*. This book was first published in 1652 and it contains all manner of cures and quaint superstitions relating to hundreds of plants. I found it fascinating – every plant seemed to have a use: coltsfoot and cowslips, nettles, mugwort, agrimony and yarrow. The first people to have lived in our cottage would have believed in these old remedies and depended on them. They would have grown some of the plants in the garden and gathered others from the lanes and meadows nearby.

The first herb gardens were made in monastery grounds where the monks cultivated a great variety of plants from which they made syrups, potions and ointments to treat the sick in their infirmary or the poor who came to their gates for help. Many of these were plants that we now find growing wild by the wayside: horehound, alchemilla, mugwort and prunella; or around the ruins of old abbeys: greater celandine, belladonna and pellitory-of-the-wall.

In Elizabethan times all the larger houses had elaborate herb gardens, usually enclosed by a wall or clipped yew hedge. As well as plants grown for their medicinal properties many more, such as violets, roses, lavender and orris, were included for the making of perfumes, pomanders and cosmetics. In Tudor times manor houses usually had a stillroom where elaborate toilet waters, scented linen bags, flower syrups and perfumed candles were made.

I decided to make a herb garden in a corner of our half-acre plot and grow some of these plants myself. Directly in front of the cottage was a low brick wall, old and moss covered, running at right angles from outside the door and curving round to the hedge enclosing a patch of grass. It was the ideal place for herbs. I could dig up the grass and plant them there. As the cottage faced south they would have plenty of sun and shelter from the north winds, with shade from the hedge, which included an elder tree – according to the old herbalists an essential in a herb garden.

When I began to dig up the grass I uncovered, to my delight, an old courtyard made of red bricks, worn and mellowed with age. Round these I planted my herbs so that they would spill over on to the bricks or clamber over the low wall and twine up the hedge.

The main problem was which plants to choose since I had room for only a small selection of those mentioned by the old herbalists. I decided to grow those which I liked in particular – lavender and hyssop, bergamot and magic cowslips, coltsfoot with their soft yellow flowers in February and Madonna lilies with their lovely waxy blossoms – and plants that would be especially useful, such as sage, mint, parsley and lovage.

I collected cuttings from the wayside, among them comfrey, marshmallow and mugwort and scattered seeds of cowslips and wild violets beside those of sage and parsley. Many of the wild herbs have an added sweetness to them – wild thyme and marjoram picked from the downs have all the pungency of those grown in the garden and something more; while the joy of picking wild violets and cowslips from a sunny bank can be relived in winter when the flowers have been sugared and used to decorate a cake. Cowslip and dandelion wine are old country favourites and apple jelly made from wild crab apples far surpasses in flavour and richness of colour any jelly made from the fruits of an orchard. Most of the plants are also surprisingly easy to grow from seed. Chervil and dill produce an abundance of flowers and there is usually plenty of flax, cumin, fennel, lovage, caraway and rue flourishing with the nettles and goosegrass.

For practical reasons with two small children I did not include any poisonous plants although an important herb in all the old gardens would have been belladonna, a favourite medieval narcotic.

I filled the top of the low wall with marigolds which re-seed themselves year after year. They make a lovely splash of colour and add flavour to winter soups and stews. One or two wallflower plants, once considered the emblem of love because they grow so constantly, add their delightful fragrance to the garden in spring, while periwinkles and forget-me-nots have crept through the hedge to invade the grassy lane the other side, and an old briar rose in the hedge sets its scarlet hips against the bare grey twigs of winter to brighten the dull days and feed the blackbirds and fieldfares.

1 Making a Herb Garden

He causeth the grass to grow for the cattle, and herb
for the service of man:
that he may bring forth food out of the earth;

Psalm 104

The choice of plants for a herb garden should be a matter of personal preference, taking into consideration the size and site available and whether it is to be a garden laid out with paths and low hedges or an informal clump of plants near the kitchen door. The most pleasing and useful garden would include a variety of plants selected for their culinary or medicinal use, or as dye plants or material for winter decoration.

Herbs need a sheltered site, ideally facing south or south-west, with protection from the drying north and east winds of winter. It is often the cold March winds after a wet winter that kill plants such as thyme and blister and brown the leaves of bay and rosemary. A light soil with some well-rotted garden compost or manure added is best. If the soil is heavy clay, deep digging in the autumn is advisable, leaving the frost and wind to weather the soil and break it down. A dressing of lime can be given to the soil and some leaf mould added. Thymes, rosemary, hyssop and sage do not like waterlogged conditions in winter but, in a hot summer, plants such as mint and bergamot will wilt visibly in the sun so some light shade in a part of the herb garden is useful. Mint will produce more luxuriant growth in a damp corner.

Informal Herb Gardens

A south-facing wall, perhaps against a house or garage, is an ideal setting for an informal herb garden. Otherwise shelter can be obtained by erecting a hedge or fence (which could be screened by a sweet-scented honeysuckle) or by planting a hedge or shrubs to act as a wind-break. Suitable shrubs for a wind-break would be the winter-flowering witch hazel (*Hamamelis mollis*), or viburnums, which add charm to the garden at a time of the year when there are few flowers. Many herbs are evergreen and will provide pleasure all the year.

In an informal border place tall plants at the back, with low-growing or creeping ones at the front of the border and medium-height plants in the middle. This may sound obvious, but without planning it is possible to find wild thyme hidden behind a tall clump of fennel, and chives obscured by a very handsome foxglove, or mullein plant.

Daisy

Tall Plants

Plants that do well at the back of the border include wormwood, tarragon, teasel, angelica, fennel, foxglove, Madonna lilies, anchusa and mullein. Wormwood has a delightful scent when brushed, but the whole plant has a bitter taste. According to legend, wormwood sprang up in the tracks of the serpent as it crawled out of Paradise. Wormwood and tarragon belong to the group of plants known as the artemesias. Tarragon, also known as Dragon's wort (wort being an old Saxon word meaning herb), with narrow leaves and spikes of small green flowers, is a favourite herb in continental cookery. French tarragon (*Artemesia dracunculus*), reputedly the better and finer flavoured, is a shorter plant than the Russian tarragon (*Artemesia dracunculoides*), and grows to a height of 2–3ft, while the Russian plant grows up to 5ft and has paler leaves. A rich, deep soil and full sun will produce the finest flavour. After some years the flavour of French tarragon tends to deteriorate. Both wormwood and tarragon are perennials easily raised from seed sown into the open ground in May.

A striking plant which grows up to 6ft high along the banks of streams and ditches and beside the edges of fields is the wild teasel. It is a biennial, flowering in the second year. The cylindrical flower-heads are composed of numerous small purple flowers surrounded by spiny bracteoles. When dried they are very attractive for winter arrangements, so if there is room at the back of the border it is worth growing one or two plants. The flowers and leaves can be used fresh for dyeing wool.

Angelica was always considered a holy herb and was thought to have been given to a monk by an angel as a cure for the plague. At one time it was grown in every garden, and John Gerard, herbalist to James I, in his *Herball, or General Historie of Plants* (1597) advises chewing a piece of the root against pestilence and plague. Angelica may be grown from seed sown into the open ground in May, but the seed needs to be really fresh or germination is slow and erratic. This is often the case with the *Umbelliferae*. Do not allow the plants to run to seed or they will die afterwards. If the flower stalks are cut as they appear, it is possible to keep the plants perennial. Angelica grows up to a height of 6ft; the stems can be candied and used as cake decorations.

Fennel, another umbelliferous plant, with feathery leaves and yellow flowers is more easily grown from seed. This may be sown into the open ground in spring. Fennel is a true perennial. It was used extensively in medieval days when cattle were killed at the onset of winter and the meat salted. To disguise and vary the taste of the meat, herbs were used liberally—the strong aniseed flavour of fennel being a favourite one. It was also used in the Middle Ages to plug keyholes to keep away ghosts. To some the scent of fennel is unpleasant, but for those who like it, it makes a lovely addition to the herb garden and is good for dyeing wool. Fennel is found growing wild and transforms lanes in late summer, its yellow umbels growing with the beautiful blue of chicory among the golden grasses and ripening blackberries.

Another wild plant, the foxglove, deserves a place in the border, being an important drug herb. Foxgloves are easily raised from seed, flowering in the second year, after which the plants die. A single plant will produce thousands of seeds and the following spring there will be enough tiny seedlings around the original plant to fill a wood.

Madonna lilies, with their beautiful, white, highly perfumed flowers, were grown in Tudor herb gardens and used for making an ointment to heal wounds. They can be added to the border for their decorative value and old-style associations.

Anchusa is a tall border plant growing up to 5ft high with bright blue flowers in April and May. The roots of this plant have been used as a source of red dye since Egyptian times. Propagate anchusa by root cuttings in autumn.

Another biennial herb that grows wild is mullein. It is still widely

A cottage herb garden

Herbs planted among brick paving around an old well

used in Ireland, where the leaves are boiled in milk and used for coughs and bronchial troubles. The plants are tall, sometimes growing as high as 8ft with thick, woolly leaves, greyish in colour, like felt blankets. The yellow flowers are five-petalled and carried in tall spikes. The stems of the plant can be dipped in wax and used for candles and tapers. There are several other species of wild mullein with similar properties. Among them is the black mullein (*Verbascum nigrum*), a smaller plant with emerald leaves and purple anthers to the yellow flowers.

Medium-height Plants

Medium-height plants could include sage, hyssop, lavender, yarrow, balm, lad's love, bergamot and tansy. Sage, a perennial easily raised from seed, was always grown in cottage gardens, being held in high esteem as a healing plant. Cottagers used to eat sage leaves with their bread and cheese. Old sage bushes become quite large and straggly and should be layered and new, smaller plants obtained. When the old bushes are discarded, cut the stems, tie in bunches and hang them to dry. You will then have a good supply of dried sage for winter use.

Yarrow was the witches' herb used in incantations and spells, but it was also a favourite of the old herbalists and used to stay bleeding and heal wounds. It was reputedly the herb applied by Achilles to staunch his wounds and the name *Achilles* was given to the genus in his honour. The wild yarrow growing by the wayside has flat-topped flower-heads consisting of numerous small flowers, usually white but sometimes a pale pink or even rose-coloured. *Achilles filipendula* 'Cloth of Gold' is an attractive plant for the herbaceous border. The flowers, in large yellow corymbs, dry well for winter arrangements and retain their colour. Yarrow is an invasive plant and needs to be kept in check by cutting back unwanted runners in March or April. It will also produce self-sown seedlings all over the herb garden, but it is an interesting plant to include.

A delightful plant for any herb garden is balm, also known as melissa, for, when brushed, the whole plant gives off a strong lemon scent. To dry the plants cut them before they come into flower, about the end of May. Plants of balm are easily raised from seed sown in May and once established they are very prolific and need to be kept in check.

Lad's love, or southernwood, is another plant belonging to the group of artemesias. Artemis in Greek mythology was goddess of the moon and the chase. Lad's love is the symbol of love and fidelity even in bitter circumstances, and country boys used to give a sprig to their sweethearts after church on Sundays. It was planted in cottage gardens to bring good luck to those who lived there. Like all the artemesias it has a bitter taste but delightfully aromatic foliage which, when dried, will keep moths from clothes in the same way as wormwood – hence the French name for the plant of 'garde robe'. A native of southern Europe, it rarely flowers in more northern latitudes but is easily propagated by cuttings. In a border the grey-green finely cut foliage looks most attractive if planted alongside orange marigolds or the emerald tansy and the bright scarlet bergamot, a plant of the herbaceous border, which makes a colourful addition to the herb garden. The leaves give off a strong lemon scent and the scarlet flowers can be added to salads. There are also pink- and mauve-flowered varieties.

Tansy was a popular herb in the Middle Ages when elaborate puddings, known as 'tansies' and consisting of cream, eggs, white wine and tansy leaves were made. Tansy has a strong, aromatic flavour which, if used sparingly, is very pleasing. The plant, with its emerald pinnate leaves and yellow button-like flowers, is useful for cooking, dyeing and decorative purposes. Tansy was known as the herb of St Athanasius – named after the fourth-century bishop of Alexandria, famed for his defence of ecclesiastical liberty against the State.

Another herb that could be included in the middle of the border, and one which would make an interesting and unusual addition, is rue. The plant has blue-green pinnate leaves and yellow flowers with emerald centres. Known as the herb of grace, it has been taken as the symbol of regret and repentance. It was thought to be effective against the plague and was one ingredient of a medieval antiseptic known as 'four thieves' vinegar' – a preparation made up of lavender, sage, mint, rosemary and wormwood mixed with camphor and vinegar – used for washing the hands and bathing the face. Sprigs of rue were carried by judges at the assizes to ward off jail-fever. The whole plant has a disagreeable smell, but rue tea is said to be good for nervous headaches. Rue is a perennial and easily raised from seed.

Low-growing Plants

There are many low-growing plants for the front of the border: prunella and alchemilla, both favourite plants of the monks and once widely grown in the monastery gardens; thyme and savory, both the creeping wild thyme – that lovely plant of the chalk downs – and the common garden thyme, and the winter and summer savories. Winter savory is the perennial and summer savory is the annual form. Both are easy to raise from seed sown into the open ground in spring. Savory is a native of the Mediterranean, where it grows wild on the hills in great profusion. It was the favourite herb of the Romans and used in place of spices.

Coriander, once famed as an aphrodisiac, cowslips, chamomile, parsley and chives can all be grown as an edging to the herb border. Chives make attractive small clumps, which can easily be increased by division, the globular purple flower-heads appearing in June.

The tubular yellow flowers of the cowslip which appear in meadows and grassy places every April and May are a familiar sign that summer is on the way and the buds usually open at the same time as the first swallows arrive. The flowers were once a great favourite for flavouring puddings and the leaves were used as a treatment for freckles.

Prunella was known as all-heal or self-heal, and thought to be a cure for most ailments, particularly for healing wounds and ulcers. This is such an easy plant to grow that it usually needs to be kept in check. A common wayside herb, prunella is also found growing in most lawns that are not entirely weed free.

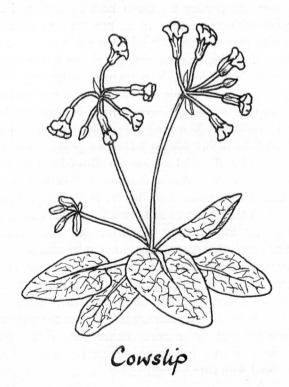

Cowslip

A favourite plant of the old herbalists was alchemilla or lady's mantle. It grows wild in grassy places and is an asset to any herb garden. The leaves are rounded and lobed with toothed edges, and when they first open they are pleated and fan-like, sparkling with the dew drops that catch at their base. The tiny yellow-green flowers resemble soft clouds at the end of branching stems.

Pulmonaria is a pretty spring flowering plant, also known as soldiers and sailors or spotted dog. It has oval leaves covered with pale spots and in the Middle Ages these were thought to resemble lungs, and by the Doctrine of Signatures it was believed that the plant was a cure for all pulmonary troubles. The flowers are pink at first, changing to blue as they mature and fade. The plant blooms early in the year, sometimes as soon as February, and is a good plant to include for this reason. It is easily propagated by division.

Another early flowering herb, the lesser celandine, a plant once used as a cure for wounds and ulcers, has glistening, yellow star-like flowers which appear in February above the bright emerald heart-shaped leaves. This is the plant of which the poet Wordsworth was so fond and about which he wrote several poems.

Many people find parsley a difficult herb to grow and there are numerous superstitions attached to it, probably on account of its somewhat erratic germination. It is said that the seed goes to the devil and back seven times before germinating and that it will only flourish if planted by an honest man. It is thought to be very unlucky to transplant parsley. It was the plant used in funeral wreaths in Ancient Greece. For success in sowing, the seed must be really fresh, as with some other *Umbelliferae*. Warming the soil by pouring boiling water over it half an hour before sowing will assist germination. Parsley is normally biennial but if the plants are not allowed to flower they will remain perennial. In a hot summer they may bolt in the first year.

Another herb for the front of the border is the Pasque flower (*Pulsatilla vulgaris*). This is the rare and beautiful wild anemone found on chalk downs and in limestone pastures, and also cultivated on rockeries. The purple flowers are borne on slender silky stems in April, and have numerous golden stamens. The leaves are deeply divided and the whole plant is covered with silky hairs. The flowers, which close in the evening, are supposed to be where the fairies sleep. Pulsatilla contains a toxic principle anemonin, which is used for respiratory and digestive troubles and for nervous exhaustion. If the leaves are bruised on the skin they can cause intense irritation, so the plant should be treated with care.

A herb garden needs to be accessible so it is a good idea to use a bed beside a path. Plants that could be used to edge the bed include the dwarf munstead variety of lavender which grows to a height of 18in and can be clipped into shape, and clumps of parsley, chives and thyme. Grow rosemary, sage, hyssop, marjoram, tansy, balm, chinese lanterns, bergamot and rue in the main part of the bed. All these herbs are perennial and the bed would be easy to care for. Collecting the herbs would keep the plants in a neat shape. The lavender will scent linen, chinese lanterns and tansy will be useful for dyeing and winter decoration; tansy and the other herbs would provide flavour for cooking. The flower bed need not be large, even a small bed with one clump of each of these herbs would be most useful. Some marigold seeds could be scattered among the other plants to add colour to the garden and spice to stews.

If you are lucky enough to have an elder tree or crab apple tree in the garden, plant a bed of herbs around it. Here you can plant large clumps of wormwood, feverfew, lovage, fennel and balm, with primroses, violets and cowslips to candy. Primroses were formerly made into puddings by frying the flowers in butter and sugar, and Disraeli was said to enjoy primrose pudding for breakfast – Samuel Pepys preferred nettle porridge.

A site sloping down to a stream or river can be a delightful setting for a herb garden. Those plants which like moister soil – mints, pennyroyal, bergamot, angelica and sweet flag – would flourish near the stream with brooklime and watercress growing at the water's edge, while other herbs could be grown higher up the slope away from the water. The leaves of sweet flag are sweetly scented when crushed, and it was used as a strewing herb for covering floors. The small pale-green flowers are crowded into a dense spike and appear in June and July. It grows to a height of 4ft and is found near rivers, ponds and canals.

A dry sloping bank can also be used for growing herbs. Plants could include wild thyme, the common garden thyme, winter and summer savory, chamomile, Spanish mint (*Mentha requienii*) and periwinkles. Spanish mint is the smallest of the mints, growing about 1in high, with a very strong peppermint scent. It likes a warm sheltered site and can also be used for herbal lawns. Chamomile, used for lawns, would spread over a bank and be delightful for sitting upon. At Sissinghurst Castle, one of the most beautiful gardens in England made by the writer V. Sackville West, a stone seat is cushioned with chamomile. This idea could be copied, building up a seat from stone and leaving a depression in the top to fill with soil and plants.

Periwinkles, once held in high esteem as herbs, were known as sorcerer's violets. They were supposed to have power over demons and the young tops of the plants were taken as a cure for nightmares. It was thought that chewing the herb stopped bleeding from the mouth and nose. The mauve-blue flowers are a welcome sight in spring. The plants layer their stems naturally, producing roots at the nodes on the stems as they touch the soil. A rooted end can be severed from the parent plant and replanted.

If you have a paved courtyard you can make an attractive herb garden by removing some of the pavings and planting herbs in their place. Parsley, thyme, hyssop, lavender, basil, chervil, catmint, chives, mint and marjoram can all be planted between pavings and in this way invasive plants, such as mint, can be kept in check. A tub planted with a bay tree could stand in the courtyard. The bay tree (*Laurus nobilis*) is the true laurel, a native of the Mediterranean. The leaves and berries of the bay were made into wreaths in Roman times for conquerors and poets. So we speak of the poet laureate – the crowned poet. A bay tree always used to be planted near a house to dispel the evil power of witches and protect the house from lightning. Bay trees can be grown from cuttings or layers but, although hardy, need a fairly sheltered position out of north winds. The cold drying winds of winter will quickly brown and blister the leaves and it is this, rather than frost and snow, which spoils the plants. A bay tree planted in a tub or large pot can be kept clipped to shape. Use the leaves, fresh or dried, for flavouring stews and pickling herrings and other fish.

A Wild Garden

If the garden is large and part of it is left as a wild garden, then this would make an excellent setting for wild herbs such as mullein, teasel and foxgloves. Cowslips could also be introduced and, once established, would produce self-sown seedlings and increase themselves. Another plant that could be included in the wild garden is honesty which has bright purple flowers in May, followed by the silvery seed-heads so popular in winter flower arrangements. Honesty is another biennial and, like foxgloves, mullein and teasels, once established will reappear year after year from self-sowings.

If you have a wild corner of the garden it is worth leaving some nettles. These familiar plants are generally unpopular, but country people cook them in the same way as spinach, and nettle tea made from the fresh tops is a good cure for rheumatism. Nettles are a source of vitamin A but have a curious drying effect on the palate. The nettle is said to have been introduced by the Romans who brought the seeds over with them in an attempt to cure the ailments they developed in our cold climate. Nettle seeds were drunk in wine as an antidote to the poisons of hemlock, henbane and nightshade and as a remedy against the bites of mad dogs.

Nettles are the host plant of some of our most beautiful butterflies – the Vanessids (peacock, red admiral, painted lady, comma and small tortoiseshell). Nettle leaves are torn to shreds in June by the dark hairy caterpillars of these butterflies, feeding in large numbers on the plants, and as butterflies are sadly decreasing in many areas due to more efficient farming it is worth leaving a few nettles in an odd corner of the garden, if only for this reason. The fibres of the nettle can be rotted like flax and spun into yarn to make a very durable cloth. The poet Campbell stated that he had slept in nettle sheets and dined off a nettle tablecloth. In the Hans Christian Andersen story 'Wild Swans', Elise spins nettles into shirts for her eleven brothers to break the spell that turned them into swans.

Two pretty woodland plants – woodruff and wood anemone – can both be introduced into a shady corner of the wild garden. Woodruff, once a favourite herb for scenting linen, is a slender plant with smooth leaves borne in whorls round the stem in a similar manner to the familiar goosegrass – so named as it was once used to feed newly hatched goslings. The tiny white flowers of the woodruff are carried in small clusters at the end of the stems. During the Middle Ages bunches of the herb were hung in houses to sweeten the air. It is not until the plant is drying that it becomes scented – with the sweet smell of new-mown hay. Propagation is by seed or division.

The wood anemone is a dainty spring-flowering plant with white flowers made up, not of petals, but six to nine white sepals delicately tinged with pink on their outer sides. The centre of the flowers are a mass of silky golden stamens. It is said that the wood anemone only opens when the wind blows, hence its other name of windflower. In medieval times the wood anemone was believed to be a cure for leprosy and a decoction of the leaves was used to bathe affected parts of the body.

One interesting way of growing herbs would be to group them to-gether according to their natural orders: plants of the order *Labiatae*, including mint, sage, lavender, hyssop and bergamot forming one

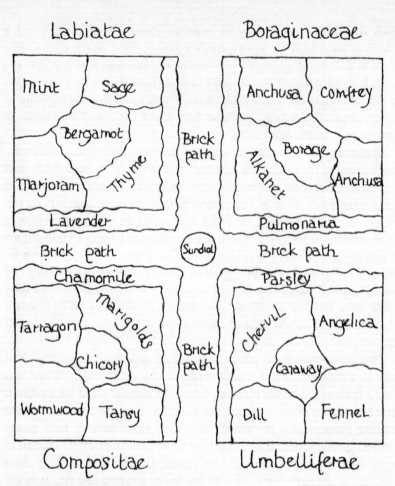

Labiatae

Mint   Sage

Bergamot

Marjoram   Thyme

Lavender

Brick path

Boraginaceae

Anchusa   Comfrey

Alkanet   Borage

Anchusa

Pulmonaria

Brick path   (Sundial)   Brick path

Chamomile

Tarragon   Marigolds

Chicory

Wormwood   Tansy

Brick path

Compositae

Parsley

Chervil   Angelica

Caraway

Dill   Fennel

Umbelliferae

group; umbelliferous plants as lovage, caraway, chervil, fennel and dill forming another; and compositous plants including dandelions, chicory, tarragon, wormwood, lad's love, ragwort and feverfew forming yet another group. There are several natural orders that can be well represented in the herb garden in this way, and the comparisons in flowers and the subtle differences in the scent of the foliage can be more easily appreciated.

Plants belonging to the order *Solanaceae* are particularly interesting. This group includes the potato, the tomato and tobacco, and some important drug herbs – belladonna, henbane and datura. Also belonging to the order *Solanaceae* are the mandrake – a plant once endowed with magical properties – chinese lanterns and nicandra or apple of Peru – thought to repel flies. Henbane is a sporadic wild plant, growing near old dwellings and sometimes seen in clumps in a chicken run,

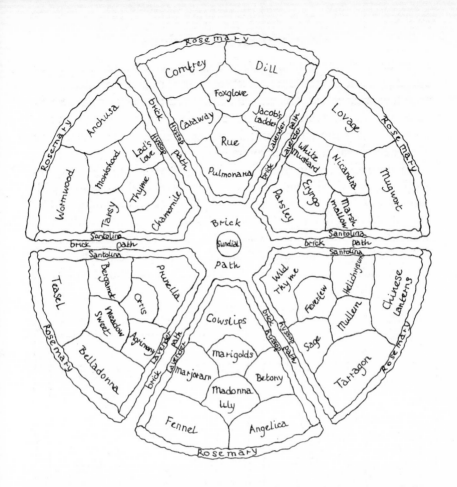

shunned by the hens, when all other green plants have been eaten – hence its name. The leaves are hairy, grey-green and the dull yellow flowers have purple veining and bright purple anthers. The whole plant has an unpleasant smell and rather sinister appearance and should be treated with care. Henbane was supposedly used by witches in their stews and the dead in Hades were thought to be garlanded with the herb as they wandered hopelessly along the banks of the Styx.

Most plants belonging to this group are more or less poisonous and have narcotic properties. The tubers of the potato (*Solanum tuberosum*) are used for food, but the green tops of the plants are poisonous, and it was thought that whoever went to sleep under a datura would never awake. Solanum comes from a word meaning to soothe; henbane seeds were formerly smoked to relieve toothache and the dried leaves of datura are smoked to give relief to asthma.

25

Formal Herb Gardens

It can be great fun designing a formal garden. One suggestion is to lay out the garden in the form of a wheel, with the spokes planted out in santolina or lavender. The central point could be a bay tree, rosemary bush or sundial, while sage, rue, marjoram, lemon balm, bergamot, borage, hyssop and tansy could fill the beds. The larger the area, the more plants that could be accommodated in this plan.

An alternative design would be to lay the garden out in the shape of a square hedged with tall lavender or rosemary and broken up with paths of chamomile or wild thyme – which can be mown and would be delightfully fragrant to walk upon – leading to the centre. Beds of attractive mixtures of low-growing plants such as thymes, summer and winter savory, alchemilla, basil, chervil, chives, pansies, violets, cowslips, prunella, pulmonaria and the lesser celandine could be planted.

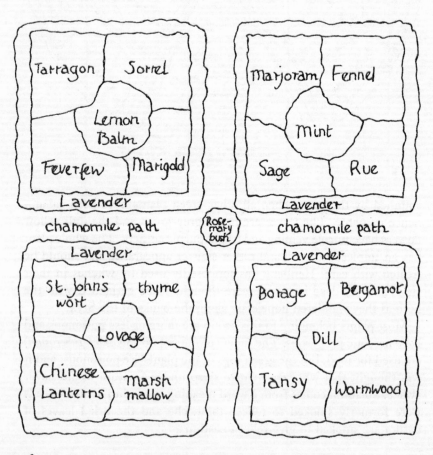

Features for a Herb Garden

Hedges

Low-dividing hedges can be used in a formal herb garden to outline beds. These can be made of lavender, hyssop, santolina or lad's love. Plant the shrubs 12–15in apart and clip them to shape in March. For these hedges dwarf munstead lavender is the best, growing about 18in high. Lad's love, unlike hyssop, lavender and santolina is not evergreen and is inclined to look twiggy and unattractive in winter. Santolina, also known as cotton lavender and French lavender, has silvery-grey foliage and golden-yellow flowers in August. The leaves can be dried and used to keep moths out of clothes. Santolina likes a well-drained soil and a sunny site. It can be easily propagated from cuttings in late spring.

For a taller divide, rosemary, which grows to a height of 4ft, makes a most attractive hedge.

Paths

Paths can be made of bricks, paving stones or plants. Old mossy bricks are lovely for paths, with plants like prunella or wild thyme spilling over on to the paths from the beds. Paths made of plants are fragrant when walked upon and for this purpose wild thyme, chamomile or Spanish mint are the plants to use. Space plants 4–6in apart and mow lightly once they are established.

Herbal Lawns

In Tudor times chamomile lawns were very popular. Drake's famous game of bowls before he set sail to defeat the Armada was played on a chamomile lawn. The type of chamomile to use is *Anthemis nobilis*. This has double- and single-flowered forms. The double-flowered form produces runners and small plantlets which can be detached from the parent stock and replanted. The single-flowered form can be grown from seed in boxes and planted out later.

When making a lawn, it is advisable to prepare the soil by deep digging to remove perennial weeds and runners. Add some compost or well-rotted manure if you wish and rake the surface level to a fine tilth. Plant out the seedlings in May, 6in apart, and by the end of July these should have grown together to cover the area. Water the young plants until established. Use a garden roller over the plants to ensure the rootstocks are pressed well into the soil. Once the plants have grown sufficiently they can be mown with an ordinary lawn mower to retain a neat appearance.

Knot Garden Beds

Knot gardens were once a feature of most Elizabethan gardens and there is a very pretty example of one at Hampton Court Palace below the window of Edward VI's room. They are formal beds planted to a symmetrical design and filled with low-growing plants such as savory, pansies, gold and silver thymes, violets and pinks. The beds were usually outlined by low box hedges.

Low Walls

Two low walls separated by a small cavity and made of dry stone can be used as a dividing boundary between different parts of the garden or used to link two levels. These walls are built up without cement, with bricks or stones from either side, tipping slightly towards the centre. Leave occasional spaces between the stones to take plants. Pack the roots with compost, push well into the crevice, push the next stone on to this and continue with the work. Pack the soil well behind the plant to prevent the roots hanging in an air pocket. Leave the top of the wall unplanted until the soil has had time to settle. A low lavender hedge can be planted on top of the wall and creeping plants, such as moneywort – once used for healing ulcers and bleeding – nasturtium or wild thyme can be planted in the crevices to hang down and clothe the sides of the wall. Marigolds planted in the top of the wall would add a lovely splash of colour and spice to the stewpot.

Spacing of Plants

Some herbs grow more slowly than others so a square foot of garden per plant is a good average amount of space to allow. For the first summer, while some of the plants are establishing themselves, the garden may look rather bare, but after this some plants, especially mints, prunella, lemon balm and tansy, will need thinning if they are not to overrun the others. Planting mint in a bucket with holes in the bottom, and sinking this into the ground, is a good method of keeping this invasive plant in check. Sage bushes, which become woody and straggly as they get older, should be layered.

Forget-me-not

Propagation

Annual Herbs

Some herbs are raised annually from seed sown in March and April. The seeds of hardy annuals can be sown in open ground but the soil should be well dug in autumn and allowed to weather during the winter before being raked to a fine tilth prior to sowing. Press the ground down a little and sow the seed thinly, covering lightly with soil. Label seeds after sowing and later thin the plants. There are a number of different plant labels on the market, the white plastic ones being quite good. Alternatively the wooden sticks that come with ice lollies are very useful. Make sure that the names are written on with an indelible pencil. It is useless to use ink which will wash off with the first rain.

Herbs that are hardy annuals include marigolds, borage, clary, chervil, dill, coriander and summer savory.

Half-hardy annuals should be sown under glass in March. This can be in a greenhouse or on a sunny kitchen window-sill. Sow the seeds in pots and plant them out in the herb garden in May. Herbs which should be treated in this way include basil and sweet marjoram.

Biennials and Perennials

Biennial plants are those that are sown one year, flower the following year and then, after setting seeds, die. Biennial herbs include honesty, mullein, angelica, foxglove, caraway and parsley. By cutting off the flower-heads as they appear, as with angelica and parsley, it is possible to keep the plants perennial, although it is worth making a fresh sowing of parsley every year. Perennial herbs that are easily raised from seed are sage, hyssop, rue, lovage, balm, thyme and fennel. For biennial and perennial herbs sow the seeds into the open ground in May. Later thin the plants and move to their permanent positions in the autumn.

Division and Root Cuttings

Division is the simplest method of propagation, but only perennial plants that produce basal shoots and plenty of fibrous roots can be propagated in this way. Large plants can be divided by thrusting two garden forks into the centre of the clump and pulling the handles outwards. Smaller plants, such as chives, can be cut with a sharp knife. After division the individual clumps should have one or more shoots and some roots. Spring and autumn are the best time to divide plants. Herbs that can be divided easily include mint, lemon balm, chives, marjoram, prunella and tarragon.

Root cuttings are pieces of root cut from the main one and replanted. Anchusa and comfrey can both be propagated in this way. This should be done in November. To propagate orris cut the rhizomes with a sharp knife, leaving a bud on each new piece of root. Plant the rhizomes horizontally with the roots pointing downwards.

Layering

This method is ideal for old plants that become straggly and woody and therefore unattractive. Make a cut with a sharp knife at a joint on the stem, cutting halfway through. Peg the cut stem into the soil and pack the soil around it. Keep watered. In about eight weeks new roots will form at the joint on the stem. The young plant can be severed from the main stem and planted out separately in September. Some plants layer themselves naturally, new roots forming at nodes on the stem where they touch the ground. Blackberries and periwinkles are good examples.

Cuttings

Cuttings have the advantage over seed that the young plants will be exactly the same in height and leaf-colour as the parent plant. But only take cuttings from strong healthy plants. There are three methods:

soft cuttings, half-ripe or heel cuttings, and ripe or hardwood cuttings.

Soft cuttings are usually taken in spring or early summer. New shoots are cut off from the main plant when they are about 3in long. Trim off some of the lower leaves and cut across the stem immediately below a joint. Dip the stem in water, shake off the excess, and then dip the end into a hormone rooting powder. Insert the cuttings into small pots of very sandy soil, water well, place in a plastic bag allowing enough space for the shoots and secure the top of the bag with an elastic band. After 6–8 weeks roots will form on the cuttings and they can then be planted. Catmint is an example of a herb that can be propagated in this way.

Heel cuttings are taken from twiggy side shoots of the current year's growth on the main stem of woody plants or shrubs. About July they will be 4in long. Pull downwards from the main stem, taking a 'heel' of the previous year's growth attached to the base. Rosemary, lavender, santolina and hyssop are all easy to propagate from heel cuttings. They will root if planted in open ground but will make roots more readily if potted up in the same way as soft cuttings.

Hardwood cuttings are made in autumn from ripe pieces of current year's growth. Cuttings between 5in and 10in long are best. Place directly in the open ground or in a cold frame, burying two-thirds of the shoot. Leave until spring. Black, red and white currants, gooseberries and many shrubs can be propagated in this way.

Herbs in a Town Garden

In a small garden or a town garden, tubs, troughs or urns look attractive placed outside doors, on balconies or at the top of a flight of steps, and window-boxes can brighten any dismal aspect.

Whatever the receptacle, adequate drainage is essential; some receptacles have drainage holes at the bottom and holes can be drilled into the bottom of a wooden tub. Cover the base with about 2in of brocken crocks, stones or weathered clinkers. On top of this spread a layer of moss or old leaves to prevent the soil being washed away. Finally, fill the container with good top soil or John Innes potting compost. The soil in containers needs changing fairly frequently and the plants will require more water than those growing in the garden. Low-growing herbs such as gold and silver thymes, wild thyme, savories, chamomile, parsley and Spanish mint are ideal for growing in tubs and troughs. A large tub can be planted with a bay tree or a rosemary bush and underplanted with thyme, chervil and parsley.

Window-boxes should be stoutly made as they have to carry a great deal of weight and are exposed to the elements at all times. Oak is the ideal material to use. Paint the outside with several coats of paint but do not use creosote as this is poisonous to many plants. The boxes should be at least 9in, and preferably 12in, deep. They should be filled with brocken crocks, moss and soil in the same way as tubs. To avoid accidents, make sure that all window-boxes are securely fixed. They can be fastened to the wall with iron brackets.

Plants suitable for growing in window-boxes are chives, marjoram, chervil, thyme, savory, parsley and basil. Mint can be added but would be better in a pot of its own plunged into the soil at one end of the window-box to avoid the runners smothering the other plants. Chives, chervil, thyme, savory and parsley seeds can be sown directly into the soil in March. Basil and marjoram (annual marjoram: *Origanum marjorana*) should be started on a sunny window-sill in pots and moved out to the window-box in May. Marjoram is a favourite herb for continental flavouring. It is an ingredient of mixed herbs and can be used in veal and poultry stuffing and with egg dishes.

A routine watering once a day should keep the soil sufficiently moist. The plants will require more water in summer than in winter.

If space is limited, small herbs can be grown in parsley pots – large earthenware pots with holes at intervals round the sides. Cover the base with a 2in layer of stones or brocken crocks and stand a roll of folded wire netting, filled with moss to aid drainage, in the centre.

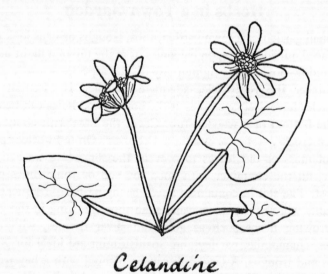

Celandine

A formal herb garden surrounded by yew hedges

Herbs growing between flagstones and planted in a strawberry pot

Press good garden soil enriched with compost or potting compost around this. Seeds should be set just below the soil surface of each hole and on top of the pot. Plant several seeds in each place as germination may be erratic and, when the plants are about 2in high, weed out the smallest, leaving a strong, healthy plant in each space.

Strawberry barrels are similar to parsley pots, but larger. Herbs suitable for growing in either of these containers are various thymes, annual marjoram, chives, chamomile and Spanish mint. As always, marigolds planted in the top make a gay splash of colour.

Another way of growing herbs in a town garden is to make a herb tree. This is done by fixing an old tree trunk or a stout pole into the ground. At intervals around this secure pots with wire. These can then be planted with small herbs such as parsley, thyme, chives, chervil, savory and basil.

Herb Gardens for the Blind

Herbs, being scented, give a great deal of pleasure to the blind and many city parks now include a special scented garden for the blind. Seats are provided in sheltered alcoves for visitors to sit and enjoy the garden. Wide paths with handrails run through the gardens and the plants are grown in raised beds. Plants that are suitable for these gardens include rosemary, lavenders, wormwood, lad's love, tansy, lemon balm, bergamot and the sweetly scented tobacco plant (*Nicotiana affinis*) which opens its flowers in the evenings. Pelargoniums, hyacinths and wallflowers should also be added. Natural shelter can be provided by sweet-smelling shrubs such as the viburnums – *Viburnum fragrans* flowering from November to February, and *V. carlesii*, which is exceptionally strongly scented and flowers in May – and *Daphne mezereum* which also flowers early in the year. These scented gardens bring a lot of pleasure to many people, not only those who are blind, and a corner of the ordinary garden could be planted in this manner.

2 Harvesting and Drying

There's rosemary, that's for remembrance – pray
you love, remember – and there is pansies, that's
for thoughts.

Shakespeare *Hamlet*

It is always better to use fresh herbs for cooking when they are available, but they may be dried during summer for winter use. Dried herbs can also be used in winter decorations and for making wall hangings. Many herbs used for dyeing will yield their colour equally well fresh or dried so if they are not required for dyeing at flowering time they may be dried and stored for use when needed.

Culinary Herbs

Culinary herbs should be harvested for drying just before they come into flower as this is when they have the strongest flavour. Sage, thyme, lemon balm, tarragon, mint and parsley should be cut at the end of May or the beginning of June. Harvest on a dry day when there has been no rain for at least three days. Cut when the dew has dried but before the heat of the noonday sun. Tie the herbs in small bunches and hang them upside down in a warm airy place – an attic which catches the sun, an airing cupboard or along the beam over an open fireplace or kitchen stove. Bay leaves can be tied in brown paper bags and hung to dry. Drying takes between one and three weeks. It is usually possible to harvest a second crop in September, especially if the summer has been wet. When the herbs are dry, discard the stems, rub the leaves to a fine powder and store in screwtop jars away from direct heat. Thyme needs care as the stems are fine and brittle. Bay leaves when dried are used whole.

To dry flowers such as chamomile, harvest when the flowers first open, usually in July. Tie the stems in bunches and hang them upside down in a warm place. For cowslips, marigolds, elder and lime remove the stems and spread the flowers to dry on racks, over a stove or in an airing cupboard, until they are brittle. This should take only a few days. Rub the petals from the marigolds when dry and store in screw-top jars.

Some herbs, such as caraway, dill, fennel, coriander and cumin are grown for their seeds. Caraway flowers in May and the seeds ripen in June. As they begin to ripen, cut the plants and tie them in bunches, then hang the bunches upside down over sheets of paper to catch the seeds as they fall.

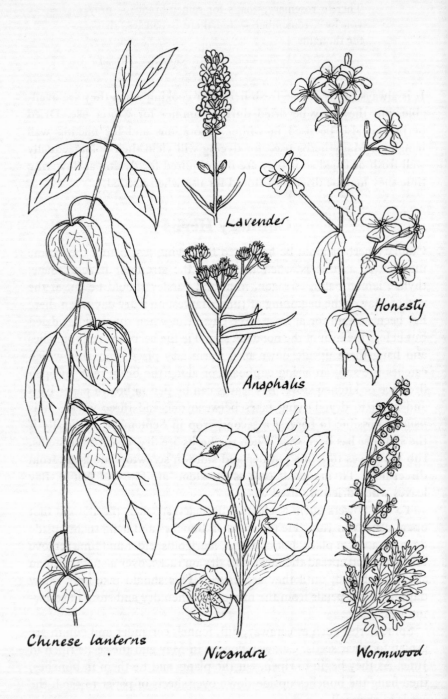

Lavender

Honesty

Anaphalis

Chinese lanterns

Nicandra

Wormwood

Berries should be used as they ripen for jams, jellies and pies and can be bottled or frozen for later use.

Roots of horseradish can be dug and used as required at any time of the year. Roots of dandelion and chicory should be dug in the autumn. After digging, scrub the roots well and dry them in the sun. Do not peel them. When they are really dry, roast them in the oven until brittle, then grind and use in the same way as coffee. They make a very acceptable coffee substitute but do not contain the stimulant caffeine. Acorns can also be roasted and used as a coffee substitute, but they are very bitter.

Decorative Herbs

Lavender, woodruff, wormwood and lad's love can be used for scenting linen bags. Pick the flowers when they first open and hang them to dry in the same way as culinary herbs. Red and crimson roses, musk roses, carnations, stocks, lavender, hyssop, geranium, bergamot and rosemary can be gathered for pot-pourris. Remove the stems and spread the flowers on racks to dry in a warm place or in the sun. Do not leave them out at night, however, but bring them in before the dew falls. The bright blue flowers of borage can be added to give colour but they must be dried as soon as picked and just before they expand or they will lose their colour.

Flowers can also be dried in sand, and will retain their shape. To do this, spread a layer of sand in a shallow box and lay the flowers on top of it. Cover carefully with more sand until the flowers are completely hidden. Leave them in a warm cupboard for about two weeks. After this time the flowers will be dry and brittle but perfectly shaped. This is a good way of preserving roses and orchids or any special flower with a sentimental attachment. Whole wedding bouquets can be preserved in this way but will need a sufficiently large box to accommodate them.

Flowers and attractive leaves can be pressed for making dried flower pictures either by using a flower press or by laying the flowers flat between layers of blotting-paper and covering them with heavy books. Leave the flowers for about two weeks. Buttercups, violets, cuckoo flower, milkwort, celandines, wild thyme, bedstraw and many small plants can be dried in this way, but it is not a suitable method for plants with thick stems or large flowers such as roses or thistles.

Flowers for winter arrangements should be cut when they first open. There are many flowers that will dry well and retain their colour such as the flat-topped flower-heads of achillea, helichrysum, statice, rhodanthe, xeranthemum, tansy, anaphalis and hydrangea. The flowers should be tied in small bunches and hung upside-down to dry in a warm airy place for a week or two.

Helichrysum, also known as strawflower, is easily grown and is a favourite of the so-called 'everlasting' flowers. The flowers are stiff and paper-like, in lovely shades of pink, yellow, orange, crimson and white. Sow the seeds into the open ground in May, or start them off earlier under glass. Cut the flowers when they first open. They will last for several years although they tend to get very dusty. Statice is another popular everlasting flower. The blooms are shades of rose, pink, blue, lavender, yellow or white. Sow the seeds under glass in February or March, prick off into boxes and plant out in May after hardening off. Cut the flowers for drying as soon as they are fully open. Rhodanthe has pretty daisy-like flowers with pink or white petals and yellow centres. They are half-hardy annuals and should be treated in the same way as statice.

Xeranthemum also has daisy-like flowers in a double form in shades of pink, rose or white. They are hardy annuals and the seeds can be sown into the open ground in March and the plants thinned out later.

The country name for tansy's yellow button-like flowers, which retain their colour well, is bachelor's buttons. Tansy is a very useful herb for cooking, dyeing or decorative purposes.

The globular silver-blue flowers of the sea-holly or eryngo are attractive in dried flower arrangements. The rootstocks are long and creeping and grow several feet into the sand. Eryngo grows freely round the coast in certain localities. In the seventeenth and eighteenth centuries this gave rise to a flourishing industry candying the roots of eryngos, which were very popular as sweetmeats known as comfits. The juice of the root was also used to soothe bites, stings, thorns and earache, and to cure king's evil.

Lavender, yarrow, larkspur, feverfew, delphiniums and molucella can all be dried for decorative use, as can the lovely sea lavender that covers saltings in late summer with a mass of purple. The wild yarrow is usually white but sometimes has pink or even rosy flowers and if dried these will retain their colour. Feverfew is a hardy annual growing 2–3ft high with aromatic foliage and white daisy-like flowers with golden centres. The plants are easily grown from seed and will re-seed themselves in subsequent years. The flowers should be picked for drying when they first open. The dried flowers can also be used as a tea for soothing nervous disorders and the plant is called feverfew, as it was formerly used as a general tonic and for fevers.

Delphiniums are beautiful perennial plants grown in the herbaceous border. The blue flowers are carried in tall spikes and if they are picked when they first open and hung upside down to dry, they will retain their colour well all winter. Larkspurs – hardy annuals, sown in March or September for early flowering the following year – can be treated in the same way.

A most attractive plant when dried is molucella, also known as bells of Ireland, which has small white flowers surrounded by large pale green calyces in long spikes. Another useful dried plant for flower arrangements or wall hangings is anaphalis, a perennial plant with soft woolly grey-green leaves and small white daisy flowers. It is also useful for providing a setting for the brighter coloured flowers in a border.

Many seed-heads such as hogweed, St John's wort, knapweed, campion, donkey's ears (*Stachys lanata*), teasels, old man's beard (the wild clematis), aquilegia, sorrel, montbretia, poppies and honesty can be dried and make attractive additions to winter decorations. Chinese lanterns should be left in the garden until the seed-heads have turned orange, then picked and hung to dry. Rub away the leaves when dry and arrange the lanterns in large earthenware or copper jugs without water. The hips of the wild rose glowing in the autumn hedgerows can have the leaves stripped from the stems and be given a spray of clear varnish. In this way they will last well for several months. Rub away the outer covering of the seeds of honesty to reveal the silver membranes. Save the seeds to scatter in the wild garden.

In any lane or meadow you can find a great many grasses with enchanting names such as canary grass, meadow grass, dog's tail and foxtail, cocksfoot, rye, squirrel tail and rat's tail, wild oat and wall barley, cloud grass and Timothy grass, all of which can be dried for decoration. If you prefer you can dye the grasses with coloured ink.

Beech leaves can be preserved with glycerine for the winter. Cut sprays of beech during the summer before the sap has stopped rising and the leaves have begun to turn brown. Split the stems with a sharp knife and stand the sprays in equal parts of glycerine and warm water. Leave for 2–3 weeks. After this time the leaves will have turned a warm brown colour and will be glossy in appearance. They are then ready to be used without water, in dried flower and grass arrangements. Forsythia leaves can be treated in the same way.

Necklaces can be made out of seeds of pumpkin and cherry stones. The stones should be washed well and then spread on trays to dry in the sun. Do not leave them out at night but bring them in before the dew falls and put them out again next day.

3 Herbal Fancies

Fetch me that flower: the herb I shewed thee once.
The juice of it on sleeping eyelids laid,
Will make or man or woman madly dote
Upon the next live creature that it sees.
Fetch me this herb,

Shakespeare *A Midsummer Night's Dream*

Dried herbs retain their fragrance and can be used for culinary, medicinal and dyeing purposes as well as in various other ways. For instance, they can be used around the home, or made into charming small gifts which are often ideal for sending to someone abroad or which can be sold to provide a little pocket money.

Pot-pourri

This is composed of sweetly scented dried flowers and leaves displayed in open bowls to give a room the fragrance of summer all the year round. A number of summer flowers retain their delightful scent when dried – red and crimson roses, damask and musk roses, carnations, stocks, lavender, geranium and bergamot. The bright blue flowers of borage can be added to give colour. Add the leaves of herbs – lemon balm, thyme, marjoram, hyssop and lavender. When the herbs are dry, crumble the leaves and mix them all together. Pack into a large jar, sprinkling a little nutmeg, cinnamon, orris root and sea-salt (obtainable from chemists), over 2in layers of flowers and herbs. Leave for 3–4 weeks shaking occasionally, then turn out into bowls.

Wild rose

Pomanders

These used to be hung in all Elizabethan houses to sweeten the air and act as an antiseptic. They have a lovely spicey smell and are nice hung in linen cupboards and wardrobes. Take a thin-skinned orange and stud with cloves except for bands at each quarter wide enough to take a piece of ribbon. A bodkin is useful to make the holes. Roll the orange in equal parts of ground cinnamon and orris root. Rub it well in, then store in grease-proof paper in a warm dry place. An airing cupboard is ideal. It should be dry and ready in about six weeks. Dust off the surplus powder and fasten narrow velvet ribbon round the bands. The orange will be quite hard and dry and will last for years.

The violet-scented orris powder comes from the dried rhizomes of *Iris florentina*. The fresh rhizomes are not scented but the perfume develops after preparation. Flowering in late May and June, the flowers are white with pale mauve shading and yellow beards. As well as being used for pomanders the powdered root is used in the preparation of some perfumes. (If you do not grow orris, dried orris powder can be bought from chemists.)

Lavender Baskets

Take 17 stalks of lavender with the flowers just opened. Tie with raffia just below the flower-heads. Bend the stems upwards over the flower-heads and weave in and out of them with the raffia until the flowers are nearly covered. Thread the end of the raffia down into the weaving with a large needle and trim off the surplus stalk ends. Make a handle of raffia and hang the basket up.

Linen Bags

Linen bags can be filled with a number of herbs and used to scent the airing cupboard or wardrobe. The best fabrics to use are natural ones such as fine cotton, linen or muslin. Do not use thick materials or the fragrance of the herbs will not be released. Cut small heart shapes or circles and fill with lavender or rosemary. Trim the edges with lace and add a ribbon bow. Lad's love and wormwood can be used to fill patchwork balls and hung in cupboards to keep away moths.

Patchwork Balls

Cut a five-sided shape – a pentagon – out of cardboard. Then use this template to cut twelve pentagonal shapes out of material. The best material to use is fine cotton, either with a small flower print, or gingham and plain colours that mix well. Stitch the shapes together with small neat stitches but leave one edge open and fill with dried wormwood or lad's love. Sew up the remaining side and attach a loop of ribbon, then hang the patchwork ball in the cupboard.

Tussie Mussies

An old custom was the giving of a nosegay, or tussie mussie, to important people who had to enter prisons and mix with the prisoners or sick persons. They were also very popular in Victorian times. Nosegays can be made from many different herbs but it is customary to have a rosebud as the centre-piece. Fasten lavender, hyssop, thyme and forget-me-nots around the rosebud and edge the posy with wormwood leaves and pulmonaria leaves alternately. Finish with a paper doily frill and a ribbon bow. Nosegays are charming for a dressing-table or for a little girl to give to someone special.

Catnip Mice

Wherever there is a clump of catmint there will usually be a cat rolling in it or asleep in it. Cats are so addicted to the plant that they will nibble it to the ground as soon as it comes up every spring. The only way to grow catmint, according to the old rhyme, is to sow seed since a small plant is nibbled away before it has a chance to establish itself:

> Set it, you won't get it,
> Sow it, they won't know it.

The leaves can be dried and used to fill muslin mice.

Cut two small mouse shapes from muslin, sew along the back and halfway up the base, fill with dried catmint, and stitch up the remaining seam. Add some whiskers with button thread, and a tail from thin string. Cats will roll about with the things for hours, tossing and chewing at them ecstatically.

Herbal Tobacco

Take equal parts of betony, rosemary, buckbean, thyme, lavender and chamomile flowers. Dry them and rub them through the hands to a fine powder. Add dried coltsfoot leaves to equal the amount of all the other ingredients and mix well together. Store in a tin and use for pipe or cigarettes.

Necklace of Pumpkin Seeds

The seeds should be well washed and then dried in the sun or in a cool oven. Thread them with a large needle and some strong thread. They can be used in their natural state or dyed. Soaking in cold tea will produce a lovely mahogany colour. After dyeing the necklace hang it up to dry in the sun. Melon and marrow seeds can be used in the same way.

Necklace of Cherry Stones

A necklace of cherry stones is supposed to attract love to the wearer and is a good-luck symbol. Dry the stones in the sun, then make holes through them with a drill or red-hot needle. Thread on strong thread. The stones can then be varnished with clear varnish.

Periwinkle Baskets

The long green runners of the sorcerer's violets make lovely small baskets and are easy to work with, being sufficiently pliable. Take six long lengths, place three one way and the other three across at right angles. Take a long runner, and loop it under the first three stakes. Using the left-hand end first, pass it over three stakes, then under the next three stakes. Then take the right-hand end of the length and, working in the opposite direction, pass it over the stakes. Using each end alternately, work round the base twice, then separate the stakes and continue, working round each one individually. When the base measures 3–4in across, bend the sides up, and insert further side stakes, one on each side of the original base stakes. Weave round the sides of the basket with further lengths until it is the required depth. To finish the top, trim the side stakes to an even length, about 3in, and taking them one at a time, bend them to the right, behind the next stake, in front of the one after that, and then behind the following stake. Work all round the top, bending each stake and weaving it down

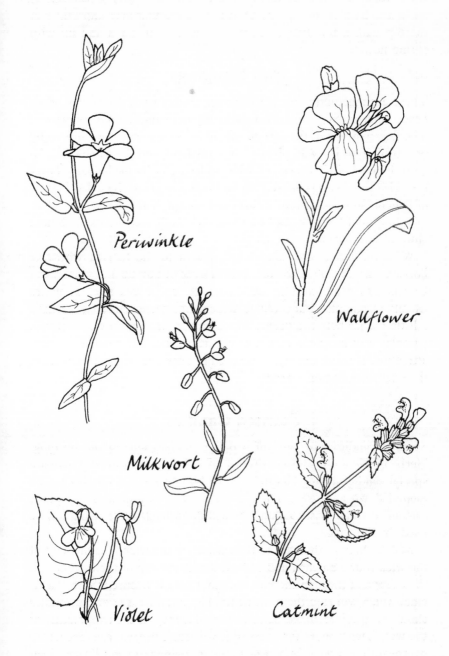

Periwinkle

Wallflower

Milkwort

Violet

Catmint

in turn. Trim the ends. To make a handle, find a thick length of periwinkle, sharpen the ends, and push them into the weaving each side as far as the base of the basket. Secure it by binding over and under at the top with a fine length. Line the basket with moss and fill with spring flowers.

Wall Hangings

These are made on a hessian backing. Collect larch cones, and seedheads such as St John's wort, wild thyme, campion and bergamot. The flower-heads of the carline thistle in the seeding stage are really beautiful. This is a wild plant of dry grassland, and the name is said to be in honour of Charlemagne who made use of its medicinal properties. Use small sprigs of wild oat and quaking grass, the dried flowers of helichrysum and xeranthemum and sprays of anaphalis. The silver membranes of honesty can be added, and single seed-heads of chinese lanterns and nicandra.

Wire the larch cones and larger pieces to the hessian with fine florist's wire or fuse wire. The small pieces of flowers and grasses can be glued in position. The wall hangings can be any size. They are usually rectangular, but could be made to fit a particular space, perhaps a little corner between beams on a staircase or over an old doorway. Circular wall hangings with a velvet base instead of hessian are very attractive. If using velvet, secure the fir cones and larger flowers from the back with button thread.

Scented Candles

Scented candles will give off a delightful fragrance while burning. Herbs to use are rosemary, thyme, lavender or bay leaves. There are special candle-making kits that can be bought but old candles can be melted down and used. There is no need to buy moulds – yoghurt cartons or small plastic containers will do instead, while string can be used for the wick.

Make a hole in the base of the carton for the wick. Tie one end of the wick round a pencil and place it across the top of the carton, pull the other end through the hole and knot below. Secure it with Plasticine, which will stop the hot wax leaking out. The wax or old candles should be put into an old pan and heated slowly. If the temperature of the wax reaches more than 200° F it will catch fire, so take care not to overheat. Tie a good bunch of herbs in a square of muslin and heat them in wax. Leave it over a low heat for 30min to bring out the fragrance of the herbs. Grate up a wax crayon and melt it with the wax to add colour. Remove the muslin and the herbs and pour the hot wax into the mould. As it cools a well will form in the centre and a little more hot wax can be added. When the wax has set and the candle is cold, carefully cut away the mould. The outside of the candle can be decorated with dried pressed flowers.

4 Culinary Herbs

> Better is a dinner of herbs where love is,
> than a stalled ox and hatred therewith.

Proverbs 15:17

Herbs are used in cooking to vary the flavour, to garnish a dish and to aid the digestion of rich food. Most herbs are fairly strong in flavour and should be used in moderation. They are best used fresh but this is not always possible, although some herbs such as rosemary, savory and bay are evergreen and may be used fresh all the year round. Dried herbs are stronger than fresh ones and about half the amount is needed, for example, if using one spoonful of fresh herbs, use half a spoonful of dried herbs. Dried herbs should be stored in screwtop jars in a dry but cool part of the kitchen away from the stove and other sources of heat and not in direct sunlight, lest the herbs lose their potency.

Herbs may be used together or singly. A recipe may require a specific herb or may use one of the following mixtures of herbs.

Mixed herbs – equal amounts of parsley, thyme, marjoram and savory.

Bouquet garni – a bunch of herbs made up of a sprig of parsley, thyme and marjoram, and a bay leaf. The herbs are tied together in a small square of muslin and added to a soup or stew until sufficient flavouring is imparted, after which the herbs may be lifted out.

Fines herbs – a mixture of herbs used for flavouring omelettes, composed of equal amounts of chopped parsley, chives, chervil and tarragon.

Herbs such as mint, savory and sage have carminative properties and will aid the digestion of rich foods such as pork. **Mint** is one of the best-known culinary herbs. There are several varieties that can be grown, all with the familiar mint aroma. Round-leaved mint and spearmint are the ones most commonly used for culinary purposes. Eau-de-Cologne mint has a slightly lemon-scented fragrance and has bronze leaves which can be dried and added to pot-pourri. Peppermint is the medicinal mint which is grown for the oil used in confectionery and in peppermint water. Mint sauce is the traditional accompaniment to roast lamb. When making mint sauce, sprinkle the leaves with sugar before chopping them, as this absorbs the oil from the leaves as they are being chopped. If using dried mint for sauce, pour 1tbsp boiling water over the leaves to bring out the flavour, and then add vinegar and sugar. Use mint when cooking peas, potatoes, spinach, carrots, cabbage or cucumber, and sprinkle over salads.

D

Mint Pasties

Mint pasties are an old country favourite.

Pastry
8oz self-raising flour
4oz fat
pinch salt

Filling
2tbsp chopped mint
2tbsp currants
2tbsp soft brown sugar

Heat oven to 400° F. Rub fat into flour and salt until it is like fine breadcrumbs. Mix to dough with a little cold water. Divide into 8 pieces and roll out into circles about 6in across. Mix chopped mint, currants and soft brown sugar together and divide between the pastry circles. Fold the pastry in half joining the edges, flatten slightly and brush the tops with milk. Bake at 400° F for about 20min until golden brown.

Mint Jelly

Mint jelly is easy to make and windfall apples can be used. It can be served with roast lamb in place of the usual mint sauce or used as a cake filling.

2lb apples
2pt water
thinly peeled rind and
  juice of 1 lemon

sugar
4 heaped tbsp chopped mint
few drops green colouring

Wash apples but do not peel and core them. Cut away any brown pieces, cut into quarters and put into a large pan with the lemon rind and water. Simmer for 30min until the apples are really soft. Mash with a potato masher while cooking to reduce the pulp. Turn the pulp into a jelly bag or large piece of scalded muslin and tie up over a bowl. Leave to drip overnight. Do not squeeze the bag or the jelly will be cloudy. Next morning measure the juice and for every 1pt of juice add 1lb sugar. Boil up with the lemon juice until setting stage is reached – this should take about 30min. (To test for a set put a little of the jelly on to a cold saucer. As it cools a skin should form over the surface.) Add the chopped mint and bring back to the boil. Add the green colouring and take off the heat. Leave to cool slightly, then pour into small warmed jars, seal and label.

Sage is one of the most useful herbs and was once used as a blood purifier. It is a well-known flavour with pork, duck or goose and is

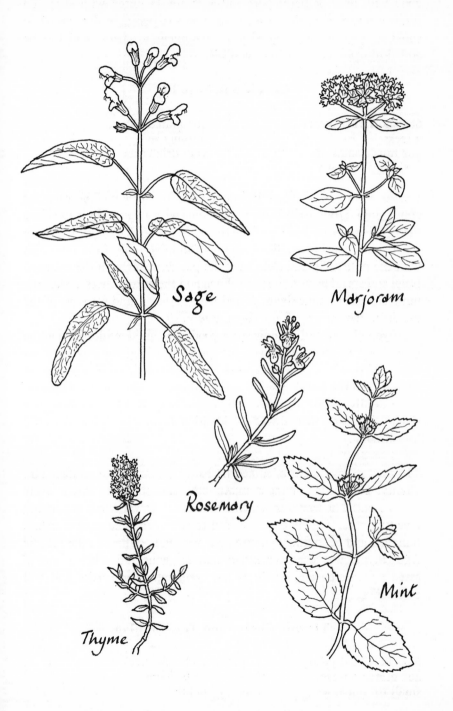

Sage

Marjoram

Rosemary

Thyme

Mint

good with liver or hare; pork sausages are flavoured with sage. To transform cabbage, add a sliced onion and 1tsp sage to the pan while cooking. Sage is also a good accompaniment to cheese and can be added to many cheese dishes and pies.

Cheese and Sage Pie

6oz shortcrust pastry	4oz grated cheese
2 leeks	2 tomatoes
4oz mushrooms or shaggy ink caps	1tsp dried sage

Heat oven to 375° F. Wash leeks and cook in a little boiling water for about 5min. Drain well. Wipe mushrooms with a damp cloth and chop them. There is no need to peel them. If using shaggy caps, choose fresh young specimens. They are plentiful in autumn. Line a pie dish with the pastry. Spread leeks over the pastry, cover with the chopped fungi and sprinkle with the sage. Then add the grated cheese. Slice the tomatoes and arrange them, dotted with butter, round the edge of the pie dish. Bake at 375° F for about 30min.

(If you plan to gather fungi get a good book on identification and be sure that you know what you are picking, asking the advice of an expert if possible. There are many edible fungi, with much more flavour than the rather insipid cultivated mushroom but there are also some deadly poisonous ones. It is far safer to go for something like shaggy ink caps that are easily identifiable than a rather doubtful 'mushroom'.)

Thyme, an ingredient of mixed herbs, is the symbol of courage and vitality. The garden thyme is an attractive shrubby plant with a lovely warm scent. The leaves are small and the pink flower-heads are greatly loved by bees. Thyme can be added to stews, egg and cheese dishes, tomatoes and in stuffing to accompany veal and poultry. In the Middle Ages thyme was used for inflammations, gout and sciatica and to assist and hasten childbirth. It has carminative properties and will ease colic.

Thyme, Cheese and Tomato Flan

6oz shortcrust pastry	16 black olives
4oz grated cheese	2tsp thyme
small tin tomatoes	pepper

Heat oven to 375° F. Line an ovenproof plate with the pastry and bake blind for 20min. Grate the cheese over the pastry. Put tomatoes and juice into a small pan with pepper and thyme and heat for about 7min, beating with a fork. Pour over the cheese and decorate with the olives. Bake for about 25min. Serve hot or cold with lettuce and watercress.

Watercress is rich in vitamin C and iron and was once the prescribed cure for scurvy. It grows as a wild plant in streams or around springs, and has dark shiny leaves that are hot and peppery to the taste. Watercress is cultivated commercially in special beds, but there is no reason why it should not be gathered wild. It is often much nicer and certainly fresher. Do not pick it, however, from streams that run through sheep meadows, as the eggs of the liver fluke, parasitic in sheep and man, hatch in its hollow stems. American land cress has the same flavour and goodness as watercress, but does not require running water and can be grown in ordinary garden soil. It can be sown in the open ground from March onwards and will mature in 10 weeks. Use watercress in salads, as a fresh green vegetable or as a garnish.

Another wild plant used for cooking which can also be cultivated is **sorrel**. It is a common plant of waste land and meadows, and the oval, bright-green leaves can be boiled and eaten as spinach or used for sorrel soup. It is widely cultivated in France and sorrel sauce is eaten there with roast fowl. Its country name of donkey's oats is hard to understand, as donkeys seem to be indifferent to the charms of sorrel. To grow sorrel, sow the seed in April and May and thin the plants to 8in apart. A rich damp soil produces the best plants.

Sorrel Soup

½lb sorrel	1tbsp cornflour
1oz butter	seasoning
1pt milk	2 egg yolks

Wash the sorrel and pick the leaves from the stalks. Chop finely and put into a pan with the butter. Stir over a low heat for about 5min. Add milk thickened with cornflour and simmer for 20–30min. Season with salt and pepper. Add the egg yolks and heat through, stirring all the time, but do not let it boil once the egg has been added. Serve with brown bread.

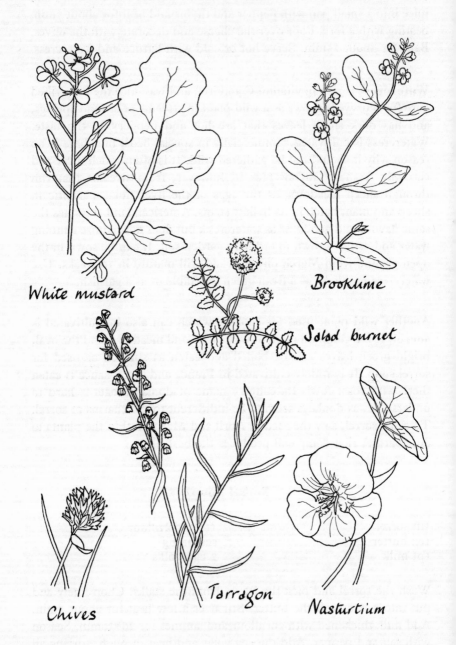

White mustard

Brooklime

Salad burnet

Chives

Tarragon

Nasturtium

Sorrel Sauce

Wash the sorrel and pick the leaves from the stalks. Put into a pan with a small quantity of cold water. Bring to the boil and simmer for 10min. Strain, chop finely and add to gravy or white sauce.

Fennel sauce can be made in the same way. After cooking, strain and chop the fennel leaves and add them to melted butter. Fennel sauce has an aniseed flavour and is made to accompany fish. **Dill**, a similar plant, is also used to make sauce for fish, and the seeds are used in pickles and herb vinegars. Fennel is a perennial, but dill, which is slightly shorter, growing to about 4ft, is an annual plant. It has umbels of yellow flowers in autumn. An extract from the seeds and roots has a tonic and aperient action, and the word dill is said to be derived from a Norse word meaning to lull.

Dill Sauce

Dill sauce is a favourite Scandinavian accompaniment to fish.

2oz butter	2tbsp chopped dill
2oz flour	1tbsp vinegar
1pt stock	1 egg yolk

Melt the butter in a small pan and stir in the flour. Gradually add the stock, stirring all the time, then the chopped dill and the vinegar. Simmer for a few minutes, remove from the heat and beat in the egg yolk. Heat through, but do not let it boil once the egg has been added.

Dill and fennel may be added to white sauce made in the same way but with milk substituted for stock and the vinegar and egg yolk omitted. Parsley sauce is made in this way, and is served with fish and also with boiled ham.

Herb Butters

Parsley, mint, chives and lovage can all be used for making herb butters. Cream 4oz unsalted butter until soft, then blend into it 2tbsp of the chosen herb, chopped. Serve with baked potatoes, steamed potatoes, carrots or spinach, or spread it on cocktail biscuits.

Chives has a mild onion flavour and can be sprinkled over salads or sliced tomatoes, added to sandwiches or cream cheese. Cottage cheese can be made with chives as a flavouring.

Cottage Cheese

2pt sour milk   2tbsp chopped chives
4tsp salt

Turn the milk into a large square of scalded muslin and hang over a basin for 24hr. Squeeze out the last of the whey and beat the curds up with a fork with the salt. Mix in the chopped chives. Serve with brown bread.

Lovage is an attractive herb and was widely grown in the Middle Ages although it is seldom seen now. It is a perennial, growing up to 4ft high which, every spring, sends up bronze-coloured shoots that turn green as they unfold. The leaves have a very pleasant celery taste and are delicious with cheese – in sandwiches or added chopped to cottage cheese – and they can also be chopped and sprinkled over salads. The seeds can be used in a peppermill instead of peppercorns. Lovage was formerly used for fevers and colic. The yellow-green flowers in umbels appear in August.

Mustard is another herb that is grown for its seeds and has been in use since ancient times. In the fourth century BC Darius is reputed to have given Alexander the Great a bag of sesame seed symbolising the size of his army. Alexander replied with a bag of mustard seed, to show not only the number of his army but the fiery energy of his soldiers. Henry VIII was very fond of mustard with roast beef and was said to have allowed his servants and retainers 160gal of mustard seed each year.

Tewksbury was famed for its mustard, which was made into a paste with local wine, put into earthenware pots and covered with pieces of parchment from unwanted letters or deeds. In Shakespeare's *Henry IV, Part II*, there is a reference to 'wit as thick as Tewksbury mustard'. Brown mustard is generally regarded as superior, and the one which gives the pungency to mustard when used as a flavouring, but it does not keep so well as white.

Mustard is a prolific yielder and may increase as much as two thousand-fold in a season. Harvesting takes place from late August onwards. The mustard seed is sent to the mill where the oil is extracted and the seeds ground to the familiar yellow flour. The oil is used in soap making and the husks are used with other ingredients for animal feeding stuffs. Mustard is often grown as a fallow crop in rotation with cereals.

56

Mustard makes an interesting addition to the herb garden. The seed can be sown in April in a well-prepared seedbed that has been raked to a fine tilth.

Marjoram is a favourite herb for continental flavourings and grows wild on chalk downs. It is a lovely plant with a delightful scent and pink to mauve flowers. It was thought that smelling wild marjoram kept a person in good health. Another name for the plant is joy of the mountains. The leaves are used fresh or dried in veal or poultry stuffing, with salads or egg dishes.

Tarragon, or dragon's wort, is another favourite continental herb. It is used to flavour soups, stews and chicken dishes and to make tarragon vinegar.

Herb Vinegar (Tarragon)

Herb vinegars can be made from mint, dill, basil or tarragon. They should last from 2–4 months and can be substituted for ordinary malt vinegar when added flavour is required.

Put sprigs of tarragon into glass jars and cover with white wine vinegar. Leave for several days, then strain through a paper filter into bottles and cork tightly. If the flavour is not strong enough, the process can be repeated, putting further sprigs into the spiced vinegar.

Basil, also used for making herb vinegars, is the enchanted herb having power over witches and used as a love symbol. It can be added to stews and is good with vegetable dishes, in particular, cucumber, peas, spinach and tomatoes.

Basil and Cucumber

1 small cucumber	1tsp chopped basil
1½oz butter	1tsp chopped parsley

Wipe cucumber but do not peel. Slice and put in a small pan with the butter and herbs. Cover and simmer over a low heat until tender, about 10min. Shake the pan occasionally to prevent the cucumber sticking to the bottom of the pan. Serve with meat and poultry.

Vegetable Ragout

1 small cucumber or 3 courgettes	6 tomatoes
	good pinch of basil
2 aubergines	good pinch of lovage

Wipe vegetables but do not peel. Slice and put into an ovenproof dish with the herbs and a sprinkling of salt. Cover with water, cover the dish and cook until tender at 375° F. This will take about 1hr.

Bay leaves are also used for stews and in pickling herrings and other fish. They can be used fresh or dried.

Soused Herrings

6 herrings	3 peppercorns
1tsp salt	12 black olives
1 bay leaf	1 small onion
6 cloves	¼pt water
1tsp mixed herbs	¼pt vinegar

Wash and clean the fish and place in an ovenproof dish. Put water, vinegar, onion, herbs and spices in a pan and bring to the boil. Pour over fish. Cover the dish and bake at 350° F for 1–1½hr. Leave to cool, then strain and serve with salad.

Salads

In medieval days salads were very elaborate affairs with many ingredients, including flowers. Violet, primrose, bergamot and chrysanthemum flowers were used, and nasturtium and dandelion leaves and flowers, as well as herbs such as lovage, fennel, mint and purslane.

Purslane has been grown for centuries as a salad herb and is a common ingredient in salads and soups in France. The plant, which grows to about 9in, has succulent fleshy leaves. Sow the seeds in May into the open ground. At one time purslane was valued for its medicinal properties and was used for ulcers, fevers and gout. **Rocket** is another good salad herb with a pleasant hot taste similar to watercress. It is an annual and grown from seed sown in April. **Salad burnet** is a wild plant of the downs, with brownish flower-heads and rosettes of dark pinnate leaves. The leaves have a mild cucumber flavour and can be used in salads or added to summer drinks.

Another wild herb that can be added to salads is **brooklime**. It has small blue flowers and dark glossy leaves, and is often found growing with watercress and can be used in the same way. At one time it was a very popular herb and, as well as being used in salads, the leaves were made into poultices for boils and ulcers.

Chervil is an annual plant with umbels of white flowers and feathery leaves which have a slightly aniseed flavour and can be sprinkled over salads, used in sauces to accompany fish, and in egg and cheese dishes. The lovely cow parsley (*Anthriscus sylvestris*) that transforms the lanes and roadsides every May is known as wild chervil and may be used in the same way. The wild chervil is rather dauntingly like fool's parsley, that poisonous snake's food (*Aethusa cynapium*) which is common on cultivated land, flowering in July and August. However, they can be distinguished by the bracteoles – fool's parsley has long, deflexed bracteoles, while those on the wild chervil are short.

Dandelion is a favourite country herb – the flowers are used to make wine and the leaves are used in salads. However, before picking the leaves it is best to cover the plants with a flower-pot in order to blanch them. Dandelions are a very useful addition to winter salads if treated in this way; used green they can be very bitter. This plant is diuretic and children are always teased about picking it. The French name for the herb is piss-en-lit.

In its wild state **chicory's** natural habitat is chalk and limestone areas but it can be grown as a vegetable to produce the blanched heads which are so delicious in winter salads. Unblanched, the leaves are rather bitter and should be cooked in the same way as spinach. They are pleasant eaten raw, chopped and sprinkled with vinegar and served with rissoles. To blanch the heads, the usual method is to lift the roots in autumn and store in damp sand in a dark place, such as a cellar, shed or airing cupboard, until the buds appear. This takes about 4 weeks. A much simpler method is to leave the plants in the ground, cutting back the tops in autumn, and covering the plants individually with flower-pots, with the crock holes covered. They will quickly produce elongated buds which may be cooked or added raw to winter salads.

Ham and Chicory

Wrap slices of ham round chicory heads and place in an ovenproof dish. Cover with cheese sauce and then sprinkle the top with grated cheese. Bake in the oven for about 30min at 375° F.

Leeks can be substituted for chicory if preferred.

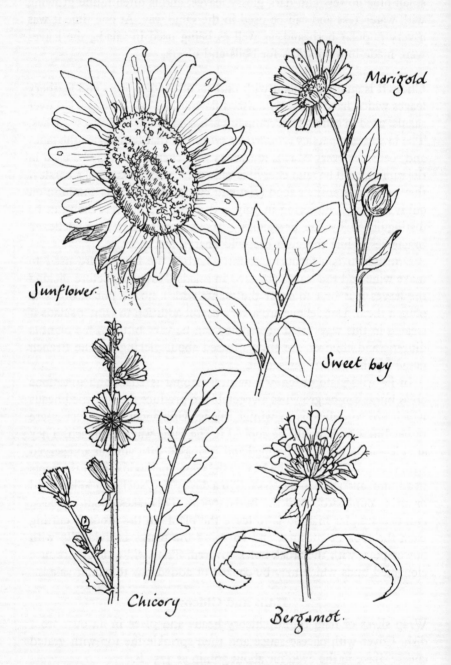

Sunflower.

Marigold

Sweet bay

Chicory

Bergamot.

The roots of **horseradish** provide the familiar sauce to accompany roast beef. They should be dug as required, scrubbed well, and then freshly grated and soaked with vinegar. The fresh roots are so superior to preparations bought in the shops that it is a pity not to make your own. Even if you do not have any in the garden, the large leaves, like overgrown dock leaves, are a familiar sight on roadsides, waste ground or railway cuttings. It is said that people have died from mistaking the roots of the deadly monkshood for those of horseradish, but as the plants are so dissimilar it seems unlikely. The plant is propagated by root cuttings taken in autumn, and though it will grow in any soil, it produces larger roots in rich, deeply dug ground.

The **nasturtium**, with orange or yellow long-spurred flowers and round blue-green leaves, both of which can be added to salads, is not the botanical nasturtium, for the true nasturtium is the watercress. It is a native of Peru, not India, in spite of its other name of Indian cress, and acquired the name nasturtium owing to the pungent taste of the leaves. Nasturtiums are easily grown annuals and do best in a light poor soil. Sow the seeds from March onwards where the plants are to flower. If they are grown in a damp rich soil, there will be an abundance of leaves which will hide the flowers. Some of the top leaves can be removed to encourage the production of flowers but do not remove too many for a plant with no leaves will die. The flowers appear from July to October and make a colourful addition to a salad. The seeds, if picked while still green, can be pickled and used as a substitute for capers.

Pickled Nasturtium Seeds

green nasturtium seeds	6 peppercorns
1pt vinegar	1tsp cinnamon
6 cloves	1tsp ground ginger

Put the seeds in earthenware jars. Heat vinegar and spices in a pan to boiling point. Pour over the seeds. Cover tightly and use in the same way as capers in sauces.

Ash keys – the winged fruit of the ash tree – may also be pickled in the same way. First, boil the keys in salt water for 10–15min, then strain and put into warmed jars and cover with boiling spiced vinegar in the same way as the nasturtium seeds. Pick the keys while they are still green and soft, the younger the better. The ash is a common tree of the countryside, with pinnate leaves and pink-stamened flowers in small racemes which appear before the leaves in March. The twigs are smooth and grey and the tree has dark sooty buds.

Pickled **walnuts** are another country favourite. The walnut was grown as an orchard tree by the ancient Greeks and is thought to have been introduced into Britain by the Romans. It makes a most attractive spreading tree with grey ribbed bark. The leaves are pinnate and a tree over twenty years old will bear drooping green catkins in May. These are followed by the fruits which are round and green at first but as they ripen the green fleshy covering rots away leaving the wrinkled shell. Walnuts for pickling should be picked as soon as they are fully formed but while they are still green and soft all through.

Pickled Walnuts

1qt malt vinegar	2tsp allspice
12 peppercorns	1tsp ginger
12 cloves	

Prick the walnuts all over and put on trays in the sun. A bodkin can be used for pricking them. Cover them with salt and turn them frequently until they go black. This should take a few days. Do not leave them out at night. When they are ready, boil the vinegar and spices, tying the cloves and peppercorns in a square of muslin. Put the walnuts into warmed jars and pour the hot vinegar over them. Seal the jars. They will be ready to eat in five or six months.

Many flowers can be used in cooking. The familiar **sunflower** is a popular cottage-garden plant growing 7–8ft high with enormous, solitary, golden flower-heads. Sunflowers are cultivated on a large scale in Europe and an oil is extracted from the seeds and used for cooking. The seeds are also grown as food for hamsters, parrots and pheasants. The buds can be cooked in the same way as artichokes or can be pickled to eat with cold meat.

Pickled Sunflower Buds

1pt vinegar	1tsp ground ginger
6 cloves	1tbsp brown sugar
12 peppercorns	

Gather some sunflower buds and wash well in salt water to remove any insects. Put into a pan of boiling water and simmer until tender –

about 10–15min. Strain and put into warmed jars. Boil up vinegar and spices and pour over the sunflowers. When cold, cover the jars. Eat with cold meats and salad.

In medieval times the **cowslip** was a favourite ingredient of cakes and puddings. The flowers can be used fresh or dried or can be preserved with sugar.

Cowslip Pudding

1pt cowslip flowers (no stalks)	1pt milk
3 eggs	pinch salt
1tbsp sugar	4oz fine breadcrumbs

Beat eggs, salt and sugar together. Heat milk but do not boil, and pour on to eggs and stir well. Blend in the cowslip flowers and breadcrumbs. Turn into a greased pie dish and place in a baking tin with hot water to come halfway up the sides of the pie dish. Bake until set – about 1–1½hr at 350° F. When cooked, sprinkle with sugar and serve hot. Half the amount of dried flowers may be used in place of fresh ones.

Preserved Cowslip Flowers

Fill the bottom of a large glass jar with a layer of flowers. Cover them with sugar, then add alternate layers of flowers and sugar until the jar is full.

Cowslip flowers can also be candied, as can many other flowers, and used for decorating cakes and trifles. Make sure that you do not use poisonous flowers. Cowslips, primroses, violets, stocks, rosemary, wallflower petals, aubretia and borage are all suitable. Avoid any ranunculous flowers (buttercups) or those belonging to the orders *Solanaceae* and *Schropulariaceae*.

Wash the flowers well in several changes of cold water to remove any insects. Shake in a clean towel. Break up an egg white with a fork and paint the flowers with this with a small paint-brush. Then dust the flowers with fine sugar and place on a wire tray to dry. Leave in a warm place overnight. Store in waxed paper in a cardboard box such as a chocolate box. Do not put into airtight tins as the sugar softens and the flowers will spoil.

Small sprigs of parsley may be candied in the same way.

Borage is an annual herb with rough leaves and bright blue flowers with black stamens which attracts bees. The leaves can be boiled and

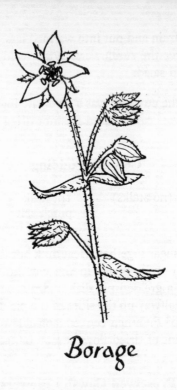

Borage

eaten in the same way as spinach; the flowers can be used to decorate summer drinks.

A plant belonging to the same family as borage, and similar although larger in size than borage, is **comfrey**. Comfrey is a wild plant of damp places, with rough, dark leaves and nodding heads of purple flowers. At one time it was widely grown in gardens, and is still to be seen in country gardens in neat rows next to carrots and onions. In medieval times it was used for healing broken bones, and its old name was knitbone. Comfrey leaves contain B12 and are cooked and used in the same way as spinach. The rough hairiness of the leaves disappears on cooking. The best way of using them, however, is to make comfrey fritters, which are delicious either as a sweet or savoury. Comfrey has been grown as a fodder crop for pigs and cattle and is thought to be a good preventive of foot and mouth disease.

Comfrey Fritters

1 egg
1 cup milk
pinch salt

dozen or so comfrey leaves
¾ cup plain flour

Herb garden for the blind equipped with handrails and with the herbs planted in raised beds

Herbs hanging to dry before an open fire

Sift salt and flour into a basin and make a well in the centre. Put egg and half the milk into centre and mix, working the flour in from the sides. Beat well to work air into the mixture. Add the rest of the liquid and beat again. Wash the comfrey leaves and discard any that have brown edges. Coat the leaves with the batter and fry in oil or butter for a few minutes on each side until golden brown. Serve hot with meat or cheese, or as a sweet, sprinkled with sugar and cinnamon.

Some herbs are grown for their seeds. The seeds of the common corn poppy are used to sprinkle on bread. Coriander seeds are used for the same purpose and also added to curries. Dill and fennel seed are used for pickling and canaries are very fond of fennel seed. **Caraway** is a biennial herb easily grown from seed sown outside in May, and the seeds are used to add flavour to pork, or in cakes. Seedy cake, as it was known, was very popular in Victorian times, but has now gone out of fashion. The seeds can also be sprinkled on bread and rolls, instead of poppy seed. Caraway was also very popular in Shakespearean days and in *Henry IV, Part II*, there is a reference to 'a pippin and a dish of caraways'. Caraway seeds have carminative properties.

Seedcake

8oz fine sugar	1lb self-raising flour
4oz butter	pinch salt
4oz lard	1oz caraway seed
2 eggs	1 teacup milk

7in cake tin lined and greased

Cream sugar, butter and lard. Beat eggs and add them one at a time. Sift flour and add salt and caraway seeds. Add flour mixture and milk, alternately, a little at a time. Turn into the tin and bake at 350° F for 1hr 50min until golden brown and cooked through.

Contrary to some country beliefs, the berries of the **elder** are not poisonous and make pleasing pies and sauces. They also make lovely jelly, either on their own or with apples. Elderberry jelly can be used on bread and butter, as a cake filling, or served with pork or turkey. The elder tree was symbolic of humility and kindness, and to dream of elder trees was a sign of wealth and contentment.

Elderberry Sauce

1lb elderberries $\frac{1}{4}$pt vinegar
1 small onion   1tsp salt
4oz sugar $\frac{1}{2}$tsp mustard

Wash the elderberries and discard the stalks. Peel and slice the onion and add all ingredients to a small pan. Simmer gently until the elderberries and onion are tender. Rub through a sieve, then return to heat until the mixture has thickened. Cool and serve with cold meat.

Elderberry Jelly

4lb elderberries   sugar
4pt water

Wash the elderberries and strip them from their stalks. Put into a large pan with the water and cook for about 30min to a soft pulp, mashing the berries with a potato masher as they cook. Turn the pulp into a jelly bag or large square of scalded muslin and tie up over a bowl to drip overnight. Do not squeeze the bag as this will make the jelly cloudy. Next day measure the juice and to every 1pt of juice add 1lb sugar. Boil up in a large pan until setting point is reached. Pour into warmed jars and seal immediately.

To test for a set put a little jelly on to a cold plate. As it cools a skin should form over the surface. Test for a set after the jelly has been boiling for about 10min, removing the pan from the heat while testing. If it is not set, boil for a further 5min and test again. Do not go past the setting point as the jelly will be thick and syrupy.

Apples were once given as love tokens and jelly made from the fruit of the wild apple tree – the **crab apple** – is delicious. Crab apples are green at first and turn scarlet as they ripen; the jelly is a beautiful amber colour. If you are planning to plant a crab apple tree in the garden, the variety 'John Downie' is a most attractive form, heavily fruiting, with a mass of blossom in the spring.

Wash and quarter the apples but do not peel them and then make in the same way as for elderberry jelly. The apply jelly can be used on bread and butter, as a cake filling or with pork.

The pale pink or white flowers of the **blackberry** are a familiar sight in hedgerows in late summer, followed by the berries which are excellent for dyeing wool. Cottagers used to bind the thatch with brambles and the long stems can be used for basket making if stripped of their thorns. The berries can be used in pies or made into jelly in the same way as for elderberry jelly. Blackberries can also be made into jam, but this is not so pleasant owing to the large number of seeds.

Fairy Puddings

blackberries	sugar
apples	borage flowers
1pt custard	

Stew blackberries and peeled and sliced apples, sweetened, in separate pans. Divide the custard between the blackberries and apples, mix each well and rub through a sieve. Put a layer of the blackberry mixture into individual glasses. Cover with a layer of the apple mixture. Top each pudding with borage flowers, fresh or candied, and chill.

Wild **strawberries** are not as common now as they once were but it is still possible to find them in woods and on grassy banks. They are much sweeter than the cultivated varieties. The alpine strawberries, now increasing in popularity, have smaller, sweeter fruits than the ordinary cultivated varieties and are nearer to the wild strawberry. 'Baron Solemacher' is a good variety, fruiting from June to October.

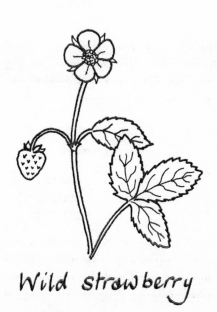

Wild strawberry

It does not produce runners and is good for jam-making, as the berries will set without adding pectin – usually necessary when making strawberry jam.

Wild Strawberry Shortcake

wild strawberries
4oz butter
2oz fine sugar

7oz plain flour
pinch salt

Put butter and sugar in a bowl and soften in the oven. Beat well together. Sift flour and salt and fold into the mixture. Press into two 6in rounds. Prick well with a fork and bake in greased tins for 45min or until pale brown, at 325° F. When cold, sandwich together with the lightly mashed strawberries, and dust the top with icing sugar. Serve with cream.

Water drunk from a well beside a **pear** tree was thought to be helpful for gout sufferers, and pears are the natural antidote to mushroom poisoning.

Spiced Pears

8 pears
½pt red wine
½pt water

6oz sugar
1tsp cinnamon

Peel the pears thinly leaving them whole and with their stalks on and place in an ovenproof dish. Mix the rest of the ingredients together and pour over the pears. Cook in a cool oven at 300° F for about 3hr until the pears are tender and deep red in colour. Serve cold with cream.

Pear Conserve

3 pears
3 apples
1 lemon

3 peaches
3 oranges
sugar

Put the fruit through a coarse mincer, and then place in a bowl with 1 cup of sugar to each cup of fruit. Stir well, cover, and leave to stand overnight. Next morning add 1 cup of water and simmer for 2hr. Pour into warmed jars and seal.

Pumpkins were the symbol of fertility and fulfilment in marriage. They are surprisingly easy to grow and can be cooked in a number of ways. Sow the seeds singly in pots under glass in April and plant out at the end of May. Prepare the soil by digging holes about 18in deep and put in a good forkful of manure or compost. It is possible to obtain really large pumpkins weighing over 1cwt. To do this leave only two fruits to each plant and cut away some of the leaves. Give each plant a bucketful of water daily. Small pumpkins about 9in across can be stuffed with herbs, cheese and mushrooms and baked in the oven. Pumpkin is delicious sliced and baked in the oven in the same way as roast potatoes.

Pumpkin and Cheese Pie

8oz cooked pumpkin, sliced
1 large onion, sliced

1 tomato
8oz grated cheese

Grease a pie dish. At the bottom put a layer of sliced pumpkin and cover with a layer of sliced onion, then a layer of grated cheese. Continue in layers ending with the cheese. Slice the tomato and arrange around the edge of the dish. Dot the top with butter and bake for 25min at 375° F.

Traditional Pumpkin Pie

6oz shortcrust pastry
a wedge of pumpkin
a handful of currants

cinnamon
brown sugar

Line an ovenproof plate with pastry and cover with slices of pumpkin. Sprinkle liberally with cinnamon and brown sugar and add a handful of currants. Cover with a layer of pastry. Cook for 30min at 425° F. Serve hot or cold with cream. This is the traditional sweet for Hallowe'en.

Harvest Frumiter

This is another traditional country delicacy and was always made at harvest time.

Put a handful of wheat grains into a stone jar and cover with milk. Leave in a warm place overnight. Next day the grains will have swollen and absorbed the milk. Serve hot with honey and cream.

Marrows are grown in the same way as pumpkins and marrow butter is easy to make and an excellent substitute for lemon curd at a fraction of the cost.

Marrow Butter

large marrow   lemons
sugar

Peel and boil a large marrow in salted water until soft. Strain, and push the marrow through a colander to act as a coarse sieve. To each 1lb marrow pulp, add 1lb sugar and 1 lemon. Grate rind from lemon and place marrow, sugar and lemon rind in a pan. Heat and boil for 45min. Then to every 4lb marrow, add 4oz butter and the lemon juice. Boil for further 15min. Put into warmed jars and seal.

Herb Flavouring Guide

BREAD, CAKES AND PASTRIES   angelica, borage, caraway, coriander, cowslips, poppy, rose petals, rosemary, violets

CHEESE   basil, chives, lovage, marjoram, sage, tarragon, thyme

COFFEE   chicory, dandelion

EGG DISHES   basil, chervil, chives, lovage, marjoram, parsley, tarragon, thyme

FISH   basil, bay, chervil, chives, dill, fennel, parsley, sage, tansy, thyme

GARNISHES   bergamot, borage, nasturtium, parsley, watercress

JAMS AND JELLIES   blackberry, crab apple, elder, mint, rosemary

MEAT

Beef   basil, horseradish, marjoram, mustard, savory, thyme

Lamb   marjoram, mint, rosemary, savory

Pork   basil, chives, elder, rosemary, sage

Veal   rosemary, sage, savory, thyme

PICKLES AND CONDIMENTS   coriander, dill, lovage, mustard, sunflower buds, tarragon

POULTRY   parsley, rosemary, sage, savory, tarragon, thyme

SALADS   bergamot, brooklime, chervil, chicory, chives, dandelion, nasturtium, parsley, purslane, rocket, salad burnet, watercress

SOUPS AND STEWS   basil, bay, chives, lovage, marigold, marjoram, parsley, savory, tarragon, thyme

TEAS balm, betony, chamomile, elder, lime blossom, linseed, marjoram, mint, nettle, sage, thyme

VEGETABLES

Beet basil, coriander, fennel

Broad beans fennel, parsley

Cabbage caraway, dill, mint, sage

Carrots basil, mint, parsley, savory, thyme

Cucumber basil, parsley

Onions sage, thyme

Peas basil, mint, thyme

Potatoes caraway, chives, mint, parsley

Spinach basil, tansy

Tomatoes basil, chives, tansy

Turnips caraway, chives, coriander, fennel

5 Country Wines and Herbal Teas

Wines

Country wines have a delicate charm of their own, especially those made from flowers. They are relatively inexpensive to make and the red ones such as elderberry or blackberry can be used in cooking.

Wines can be made from the fruits, flowers, leaves or roots of most non-poisonous plants; the best-known wines being cowslip, rhubarb and parsnip. Cider is easy to make and is a good way of using up a surplus of apples that would otherwise be left to rot. Mead is a very potent drink made with honey and was thought to be the drink of the gods.

Wine-making equipment, such as bottles, jars, corks and sterilising tablets, can be bought from most chemists and wine-making shops. Always use fresh, ripe fruit and pick flowers when they first open. Discard any berries that are unripe or mildewed as they will spoil the wine. If making wine from flowers, do not add any stalks as this will make the wine bitter.

All equipment for home wine-making should be scrupulously clean and be made of glass or earthenware. Large polythene buckets can be used for making the 'must' but they should be rigid and not the kind which softens on heating lest the addition of boiling water to the fruit or flowers ends in disaster. Polythene does not react with the wine and is easy to clean. Do not use metal containers as acid in wine can dissolve the metal to make poison and do not use crocks or bowls with cracked surfaces as the cracks can harbour bacteria. The containers should always be kept covered, either with a lid or with a clean tea-towel, to prevent fruit flies getting into the must.

After the must has been left to stand for the required time – usually about three days – it is put into large jars or crocks to ferment. Glass jars are easy to clean and have the advantage that one can see what is happening. Fermentation locks can be bought to fit into the neck of the jars. They are inexpensive to buy and prevent air and flies getting into the wine. Fresh air oxidises the wine and turns it to vinegar.

After fermentation has ceased the wine is siphoned into bottles. Any wine bottles can be used but they must be perfectly clean. Wash well in several changes of hot soapy water and then rinse in clear water. Sterilise with chemical sterilising tablets dissolved in water, leaving the solution in the bottles for several hours. Corks should be new and straight-sided; they can be purchased from chemists.

Wine that is properly made should clear itself. After fermentation ceases, sediment will settle at the bottom of the bottles. Rack – that is syphon off – the clear liquid into clean bottles. Most wine improves with keeping and if it is left to mature in large jars or casks the results will be better.

Liqueurs can be made by soaking fruit in spirits such as gin or brandy. These are relatively simple to make as the alcohol inhibits fermentation and the fruit cannot go bad. Traditionally, damsons and sloes are used with gin and blackberries with brandy, though I think the brandy is better as it is!

The dandelion is a common plant of roadsides and waste places. The bright yellow flowers appear throughout the summer, but are seen mostly in May when they make bright patches everywhere. This is the time to pick them for wine-making.

Dandelion Wine

4qt dandelion flowers	1 orange
1gal water	1 lemon
3½lb sugar	3tsp dried yeast

Boil the flowers and water together for 1hr. Grate the rinds of the lemon and orange, and put the grated rind in a large container with the sugar. Strain the hot liquid on to the sugar. Put the yeast and 1tsp sugar into a small bowl with a little warm water and leave to 'work'. When the liquid in the container has cooled to blood heat, add the yeast, cover and leave to stand for 4 days, stirring daily. Strain into fermentation jar, adding juice of orange and lemon. Put fermentation lock into jar and leave to ferment. When fermentation ceases, rack and bottle.

Elderflower Wine

Elderflower wine has a lovely light sparkling quality and is one of the easiest wines to make and also one of the pleasantest to drink.

Enough elderflowers to fill quart jug when pressed down	2tbsp white vinegar
	juice and rind of 1 lemon
1½lb sugar	1gal water

Put all the ingredients into a tub, squeezing the juice of the lemon and then adding the rind. Leave for 24hr, then strain and bottle. It will be ready in 3 weeks but improves with keeping.

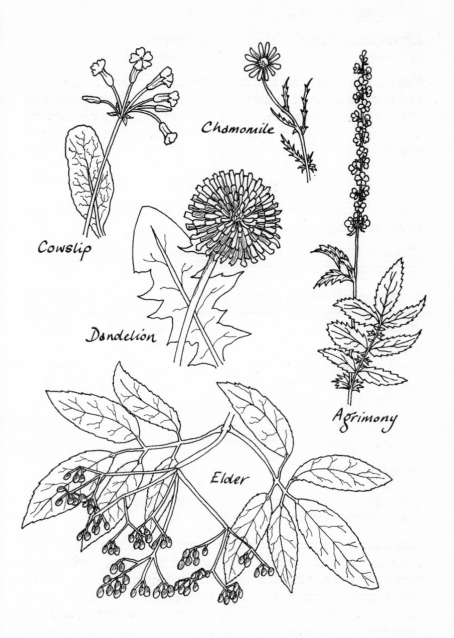

Chamomile

Cowslip

Dandelion

Agrimony

Elder

Cowslip Wine

Cowslip wine was thought to be a good remedy for colds and helpful and soothing for measles.

4qt cowslip flowers   3lb sugar
1gal water   juice and rind of 1 lemon

Simmer sugar and water in a pan for 30min. Put thinly peeled lemon rind into a crock and pour the boiling syrup over it. Allow to cool, then add cowslip flowers and lemon juice. Leave to stand for 2 days, stirring daily, then strain into a cask. When fermentation ceases, rack and bottle.

Gooseberry Wine

Sparkling gooseberry wine is another country favourite, with a taste similar to champagne.

3lb gooseberries   3lb sugar
1gal boiling water   3tsp dried yeast

Wash, top and tail gooseberries and put into a crock. Pour in the boiling water and mash the gooseberries. Add the sugar and stir until dissolved. Put yeast and 1tsp sugar into a bowl with a little warm water to work. When liquid has cooled to blood heat, add yeast and stir. Leave to stand for 3 days stirring daily. Strain into a cask and leave until fermentation ceases. Then rack and bottle. It will be ready to drink in 10–12 months.

Elderberry Wine

5lb elderberries   1 lemon, sliced
1gal boiling water   6 cloves
3½lb sugar   3tsp dried yeast
2tsp ground ginger

Strip elderberries from their stalks and put into a tub. Add the boiling water and mash the berries. Leave covered for 3 days, stirring daily. Strain into a pan. Add the sliced lemon and spices. Bring to the boil and simmer for 10min. Put sugar into jar, leave the liquid to cool slightly then strain over the sugar. Put yeast and 1tsp sugar into a bowl with a little warm water to work. When the liquid has cooled to blood heat, add the yeast and stir. Put fermentation lock into neck of the jar. When fermentation ceases, rack and bottle.

Marrow Rum

Marrow rum is made from a large marrow filled with sugar and left to ferment. Cottagers used to have one of these large marrows hanging from a tree in the garden, which no doubt attracted many wasps. The resulting liquid must have been a mixture of fermented marrow, sugar and wasps, but this did not seem to impair the flavour.

To make marrow rum select a large thick-skinned marrow. Cut the top off and scoop out the seeds from the centre. Fill the marrow with demerara sugar. Mix 2tsp yeast with 2tbsp warm water and pour it over the sugar and into the marrow. Tape the top on to the marrow and tie it cut-end up in a large piece of muslin which should be hung in a warm place for about 3 weeks. Then make a hole in the bottom end of the marrow and let the liquor run into a fermentation jar. Put an air lock into the neck of the jar. Leave to ferment, then rack and bottle as usual.

Parsnip Wine

5lb parsnips	2 lemons
1gal boiling water	2tsp dried yeast
3lb sugar	

Scrub and slice the parsnips and boil them in the water until tender. Grate the lemon rind and place in a stone jar with the sugar, parsnips and water. Mix the yeast as for dandelion wine and when the mixture has cooled to blood heat add the yeast and the juice of the lemons. Cover and leave to stand for 24hr, then strain into fermentation jars. When fermentation has ceased, rack and bottle.

Rhubarb Wine

6lb rhubarb	1 orange
1gal boiling water	1 lemon
3½lb sugar	3tsp dried yeast

Hammer the rhubarb stems to soften them and put them in a container with the grated rind of the lemon and orange. Pour 1gal boiling water over it and leave the mixture to stand for 10 days, stirring daily. Put the sugar and the juice of the lemon and orange in a fermentation jar with an air lock and strain the mixture on to this. When it stops bubbling, rack and bottle.

Beer

Home-brewed beer can be better than anything you may buy. It is easy to make and is ready to drink in about 2 weeks. The hops can be grown and dried at home or purchased from a chemist. Hops are quick-growing and attractive plants that can be trained over a shed or fence, or can be grown on poles in the vegetable garden. The common hop is *Humulus lupulus*. The seeds should be sown under glass in March or April or into open ground in May. The plants will reach a height of about 10ft by the end of the summer.

1½oz dried hops	2gal water
2lb malt extract	3tsp dried yeast
1½lb brown sugar	

Put the dried hops and 1gal of water in a pan and boil for 30min, then cool. Stand the jar of malt in some hot water to warm it, as this will make it easier to pour from the jar. Put sugar and malt into a large container. Strain the hop juice over. Add 1gal water and stir until the ingredients are dissolved. Put yeast in a small bowl with 1tsp sugar and a little warm water to 'work'. When the liquid in the container has cooled to blood heat, add the yeast, cover and leave to stand for 9 days. After 9 days pour the liquid into screwtop bottles to within 2in of the neck and add 1tsp sugar to each bottle. Screw up the tops and leave for 4 days, after which time the beer will be ready to drink.

Cider

Apples for cider making should be really ripe. They should be left on the trees until they are mature or collected from the ground and left in a pile for about 3 weeks to mellow. Chop the apples roughly and put them through a fruit press. An old wooden mangle can be used if the apples are first put into a clean linen or hessian bag. Make sure the apples are fed through the mangle evenly, or there will be a mass left at the end of the bag and the bag will burst. Put the apple juice into fermentation jars with an air lock and leave. Fermentation should take 6–8 weeks. Siphon off into a clean jar. The cider is then ready to drink.

Sloe Gin

Sloes are the fruit of the blackthorn tree – a shrub of hedgerows and common land, with starry white blossoms in March and purple black fruits in autumn. The flowers are a beautiful sight in spring, pure white with rose-pink stamens, and appear on leafless branches. The cold days of March are sometimes called 'blackthorn winter'.

To make sloe gin, the berries should be collected when they are really ripe. Green sloes will make the gin bitter. Prick them all over with a darning needle and half fill wine bottles with the sloes. Add 3oz sugar to each bottle and fill up with unsweetened gin. Cork the bottles well and shake every few days. Leave for 3 months, after which time strain the gin into clean jars and keep corked until required.

Mead

Mead has been famed as an aphrodisiac since ancient times.

3lb honey	sprigs of rosemary, balm,
1gal water	thyme and marjoram
1 lemon, sliced	12 cloves
2tsp yeast	

Tie the herbs and cloves in a muslin square. Boil the water and honey. Put into a large earthenware tub with sliced lemon and the spice bag. When cool add the yeast. Cover the cask and allow to ferment in a warm place. When fermentation ceases bottle and cork. Leave for at least 12 months before drinking.

Herbal Teas

Herbal teas are soothing and refreshing and at one time were a recognised form of herbal medicine. They are very popular in France where they are known as 'tisanes'. French peasants still drink agrimony tea as a table beverage. In medieval times beer or wines were drunk with every meal, 'small beer' – a mixture of half beer and half water – being given to children. Boys at public schools started their day at 7 am with a mug of small beer and a slice of bread. Tea as we know it – imported from India and China – and coffee were unknown in the England of the Middle Ages, and teas were made from the plants growing in the garden or gathered from the lanes and hedgerows.

Always use an earthenware or china tea pot, never a metal one as this will spoil the flavour. The herbs may be used fresh or dried. Use 3tsp fresh crushed leaves or flowers to each 1pt water. Put herbs into the warmed pot and add boiling water. Leave to stand for a few minutes, then drink, sweetened to taste, without milk. If the herbs are dried use a smaller quantity. The following herbs are all commonly used for tea: mint, lime-blossom, lemon balm, chamomile, elderflowers agrimony, thyme and marjoram.

Tea for Tiredness and Headaches

Lime-blossom tea is a good cure for tiredness and depression. The fragrant flowers of the lime open in late June or early July and if you stand near a lime tree in flower you will hear a steady hum from the bees that swarm over the blossoms. Lime-blossom honey is considered to be one of the finest. The flowers should be dried if used for tea. The lime is a very long-lived tree, living for as much as five hundred years. It does not bear flowers until it is about forty years old. The wood is not very durable and so is not used for construction purposes, but is very popular for carving, and the beautiful and famous carvings of Grinling Gibbons that adorn many churches, were carved from lime wood.

Betony, a wild herb of waysides and woodlands, is another good herb for headaches. The leaves should be dried and used for tea.

The dried leaves of marjoram used for tea are supposed to cure melancholy, soothe headaches and generally revive one's spirits. It was thought that smelling wild marjoram often kept a person in good health and bright spirits.

Chamomile tea, also good for colds, is reviving and soothing for depression and tiredness. Use the dried flowers.

Tea as an Aid to Digestion

Both mint and chamomile tea drunk after a heavy meal will aid digestion. Sage and ginger tea (page 106) is very good for colic.

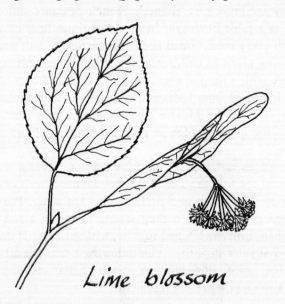

Lime blossom

Wild fruits can be used for making jam and jelly

Spinning in a cottage garden

Tea for Rheumatism

Tea made from nettle tops is still used in the country to ease rheumatism. Use 1oz nettle tops to 1pt boiling water. Take a wine-glassful frequently.

Tea for Colds and Influenza

Chamomile tea is the old-fashioned remedy for colds and influenza. Drunk when the cold first begins, it is thought to be very helpful. Elderflowers and feverfew flowers dried can also be used for colds and fevers.

Teas to Aid Childbirth

The most popular herb thought to ease childbirth is flax. The seeds of flax, known as linseed, are made into a tea and drunk regularly during pregnancy. Linseed tea is made with 2tbsp whole linseed in a jug with a sliced lemon and 1pt boiling water. Sweeten to taste with honey, stir well, cool and then strain. Linseed oil, used for sprains and bruises, is also thought to make the coat of dogs more silky and lustrous and is sometimes given to them daily prior to exhibiting them in shows, to improve their appearance.

Raspberry leaf tea is also believed to be helpful for childbirth if taken during pregnancy.

Wormwood tea used to be a favourite tonic but is not really to be recommended as wormwood contains santonin which, if taken on an empty stomach, can be toxic and cause hallucinations and confused vision.

Elder Rob

This makes a very pleasant drink for children. Put 2 handfuls of elderberries into a jug with 2tbsp honey and a sliced lemon. Add boiling water and stir well. Leave to cool, then strain through a sieve. This is soothing for a sore throat. A good hot drink can be made for sore throats from elderberry jelly (page 66). Put 2tsp elderberry jelly into a mug with 1tsp honey and fill up with boiling water. Leave for a minute, then sip slowly.

6 Natural Dyes from Herbs

> There's fennel for you, and columbines.
> There's rue for you, and here's some for me;
>
> Shakespeare *Hamlet*

Natural dyes have a lustre and beauty that far surpasses any chemical dye and the faintly aromatic smell imparted to the wool by the lichens and many plants is most pleasing. Until the sixteenth century all dyeing in Britain was done with the natural dyes of the countryside, with the result that beautiful, soft colours are a feature of medieval paintings and tapestries. The Ancient Britons used woad (*Isatis tinctoria*) to produce a blue dye for staining their bodies and dyeing their clothes. Woad, madder and weld were the three most important dye plants in the Middle Ages. In the sixteenth and seventeenth centuries the new trade routes that were opening up from Europe to America and India brought many new dyestuffs to European dyers and following French and Flemish influences the new foreign dyes were used rather than the natural dyes of the countryside. Lichens are still in use for dyeing wool in the Shetlands, Orkney, Northern Ireland and the Hebrides. The characteristic smell of Harris and Donegal tweed is imparted by the boiling lichens.

Wool is the easiest fibre to dye. Most natural dyes yield better colours if used with wool. The fibres of cotton and linen are tough and difficult to dye well and the result is apt to be patchy owing to uneven absorption of the dye. The molecules of dyes and mordants bind more easily to the animal tissue of wool than they do to the celluloid constituents of plant cells.

In this modern world of machines and man-made fibres, many people are discovering the pleasure and satisfaction of spinning and natural dyeing. It is a rewarding pastime and there is great pleasure in wearing something you have not only knitted yourself, but spun and dyed as well. Spinning is a very relaxing and soothing occupation, ideally suited to winter evenings before a log fire.

It is possible to obtain fleece at shearing time from a local farmer. This is the best way to buy it, and one can often go along and select the fleece on the sheep and watch the shearing. Once word gets round that you wish to obtain fleece it is surprising how many sources will become available. If you have the space, you could always keep a sheep yourself. But find out something about them first and inquire whether there is a local shepherd who will offer advice in times of need and be able to shear the creature for you. Sheep can become surprisingly affectionate and would certainly make a useful pet.

The origin of spinning dates back to very early times and, starting with the primitive forms of hand spinning, it has gradually developed into the commercial industry of machine spinning.

There are two methods of hand spinning. The first method with a spindle is the older form, but is rather a tedious way of obtaining a large quantity of yarn. The spindle consists of an upright stem with a hook at one end and a point at the other. A wooden disc is fixed a few inches above the point. The spindle is twisted with the hand, drawing up the fleece and letting it wind on to the spindle.

The easier way of hand spinning is with a wheel. You may find an old spinning wheel in an antique shop, but if you are seriously considering using a wheel you would do better to buy a new one. It may seem a rather pleasant and romantic idea to use a spinning wheel that is old and worn but you may be sure that if it is old, it will also most likely be warped, so that the wheel runs unevenly, and it may have parts missing. What should be a soothing occupation can end up as nothing but frustration and disappointment.

It is a good plan to practise treadling before starting to spin, to obtain the regular motion necessary. Turn the wheel to the *right*. Tie a length of wool on to the bobbin and pass it across the hooks on the flyer, which guides the wool on to the bobbin. Thread the wool through the eye of the spindle and out through the hole in its end. A small piece of bent wire is useful for this purpose. Take some fleece, pull out a little with the fingers and hold it over the end of the wool with the finger and thumb of the left hand. Turn the wheel slowly and let the wool twist, thus making a join. Gradually pull out the fleece with the right hand, guiding it through the left finger and thumb, and it will twist up and wind over the flyer and on to the bobbin. As one part of the bobbin becomes full, move the threads from the hooks of the flyer on to hooks opposite an empty section of the bobbin. When the bobbin is full, wind it off.

Do not try and make the thread too fine at first, as it is more likely to break. With practice it will be possible to obtain thread as fine as cotton, but a beginner should not aim for this. Do not worry about uneven yarn, as this makes the finished article more attractive and gives it a charm lacking in machine-manufactured garments.

Two-ply wool is more suitable for knitting as it will be stronger and withstand wear better. To make two-ply wool, thread two ends of yarn together through the spindle eye and on to the bobbin. This time turn the wheel to the *left* and let the two threads twist up together guiding them through the fingers of the left hand.

Wind the finished yarn into skeins. These should be tied in about four places to prevent them coming undone during washing and dyeing. Do not tie too tightly or there will be places where the dye has not penetrated. Wash well, at least twice, in really hot soap flakes until the wool is clean. Then rinse well in several changes of water. The wool may now be mordanted ready for dyeing, or hung to dry.

Long-stapled wool is most suitable for hand spinning. This includes wool from Shropshire, Lincolnshire and Leicester sheep. South Downs and Shetland wool is not so long, but is softer. The long-stapled wool will wear better, but the soft wool is more pleasant for articles such as scarves.

Before spinning, the wool should be carded. Gently pull pieces of fleece apart with the fingers so that the dirt and pieces of twig will drop out. Form the fleece into a rope, known as a rolag, by pressing the teased lumps together between the hands and working it into a long roll, and it is then ready for spinning. It is usual to spin the wool before washing as the natural grease present in the fleece makes the fibres twist and adhere to each other. If the fleece has been washed first it will be necessary to work some olive oil into it before spinning. It is also possible to spin the fur of other animals into yarn, notably some long-haired dogs such as sheepdogs and St Bernards. A little olive oil worked into the fur will make spinning easier.

If you do not spin your own wool, the natural Aran type wool purchased from shops is very suitable for experimenting with natural dyes. Choose natural rather than white. The average fleece weighs between 4 and 5lb, and can be bought quite cheaply from a farmer.

There is a wide range of colours to be obtained from common plants and trees, from yellow to gold, pink, orange and brown to purple. Never be afraid to try out different plants, even if they may look unlikely subjects to use as dye plants. It is always worth experimenting and it is exciting to find new colours and dye plants. Some can be quite unexpected, for example, the lovely pale turquoise obtained from the corn poppy, or the deep golden brown from silver birch leaves.

Use small skeins for test dyes and label them with the names of the mordant, dye plant and date. The dye from plants will vary according to the time of year – some dyes being stronger in spring, others in autumn. Plants that have run to seed are no good for dyeing unless you are using the roots. The type of soil will also alter the colour. Two plants of the same species growing in different locations will give a variation in colour. The usual amount of dyestuffs is 1lb roots, flowers, leaves, bark or berries to 1lb wool.

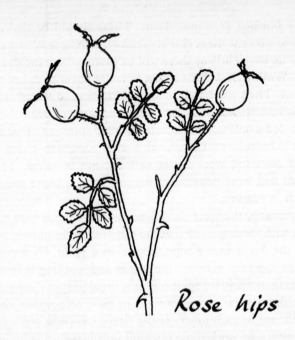

Rose hips

Generally the colour is brighter from fresh plants but this is not always the case. Weld (*Reseda luteola*) is one plant that yields its colour equally well fresh or dried. Cut the plants when they first come into flower and tie in loose bunches. Hang upside down to dry in a warm place or outside in the sun. Lichens can be spread on newspapers to dry in the sun. However, remember to bring them in at night before the dew falls. If they are at all damp when stored they will become mouldy and will be useless for dyeing. Once dried they can be kept for years. Never gather plants indiscriminately, taking all from one place, but leave as many as you pick so that they may replenish themselves. If collecting bark, do so sparingly from one side of the tree only. *Never* strip bark in a ring round the tree, or the tree will die.

The ideal place for dyeing is a special room, such as an outhouse or scullery, with a small copper fitted in one corner. Coppers, with a special place underneath for lighting fires to heat the water and a tap at the bottom for emptying the water, were once an essential feature of farm kitchens. Dyestuffs and mordants can be stored in such a room; bark and dried weld or lichens can be kept in large bags hung on hooks on the wall.

If there is no outhouse or shed available, large galvanised iron pots should be used, the larger the better, and heated on the kitchen cooker. Keep separate pots for cooking and dyeing. Dyeing can also be done in a washing machine. This will need scrubbing out well afterwards if the next wash is not to be tinted as well. Rubbing salt round the side of the drum will help to remove any colour stains. Plain wooden sticks are useful for lifting the skeins in and out of the water. If the sticks become badly stained they should be discarded or the wool may become stained during dyeing with a different colour.

Mordanting

Mordants are chemical additives that ensure that the dyes are absorbed by the wool and also assist in making the dyes fast to light and washing. They can be purchased quite cheaply from chemists. Mordants should be kept labelled and on a high shelf out of the reach of children as some are poisonous and, like any chemical, can cause skin irritation. It is advisable to wear rubber gloves when mordanting and dyeing. Never put mordants into bottles such as soft drink bottles that may be attractive to children.

Make sure mordants are properly dissolved before the wool is added, or the mordanting will be uneven and consequently the dyeing will be patchy. Below is a list of mordants most commonly used.

Alum (potassium aluminium sulphate)

This mordant produces the lightest shades, least fast to light. It has been used by dyers since ancient times. It is usually used with cream of tartar, as this brightens and evens the colour. For every 1lb wool use 3oz alum and 1oz cream of tartar. Make sure that the pot is large enough – there should be enough room to cover the wool with water and to move the wool about. Dissolve the alum and cream of tartar in the water and heat. As the water warms, add the wool and bring gradually to boiling point. Then turn down the heat and let the wool simmer for $\frac{3}{4}$hr. Lift the wool out of the water and drain for a moment. Then squeeze the water out gently but do not wring. The wool may be dyed immediately but it is better left for 24hr. Do not wash the wool after mordanting with alum, but keep it damp in a linen bag until it is dyed.

Chrome (bichromate of potash)

A chrome mordant produces good bright colours fast to washing and light and gives a soft and silky feel to wool. Chrome is sensitive to light so a lid should be kept on the pot while mordanting, or the resultant dyeing may be patchy and uneven. Mordant with chrome before dyeing in the same way as with alum, using about $\frac{1}{2}$oz chrome. Chrome is bought as bright orange crystals which should be treated with care for they can cause skin irritation. After mordanting, wash the wool well and keep in a linen bag until ready for dyeing.

Iron and Copper (ferrous sulphate and copper sulphate)

Iron gives dull, dark shades, fast to washing, while copper gives greenish shades which are fast to light. When using these mordants first dye the wool and then add the mordant to the dye bath. Too much iron makes the wool hard.

Simmer the wool for about 30min with the dyestuff. Then remove the wool from the pot. Dissolve the mordant – about $\frac{1}{2}$oz of either for each 1lb wool – and 1oz cream of tartar, and stir them into the dye bath. When it is well mixed, return the wool and continue. An iron mordant will give a dramatic change of colour. For example, when using blackberry shoots, after boiling for 30min with the wool, the liquid is milky in colour and the wool unchanged. As soon as the iron is added, the wool turns black. Copper can be added to a dye bath of yellow to produce attractive green shades.

Tin (stannous chloride, crystals of tin)

Tin is used to obtain the brightest colours, especially red and yellow. It is fast to light and washing. Too much tin will make the wool harsh and brittle.

The wool is mordanted with tin before dyeing in the same way as with chrome and alum. Use $\frac{1}{2}$oz tin crystals and 2oz cream of tartar for 1lb wool. Tin should be carefully dissolved before putting into a pot made of galvanised iron, as tin destroys the surface.

Dyeing

It is essential to dye enough wool for the intended garment at one time as it is virtually impossible to match the colour a second time. Make sure that the pot is large enough to take the wool and the dyestuff.

Flowers and Leaves

Use 1lb flowers or leaves to 1lb wool. You may find it easiest to tie the flowers in muslin first. Put into the pot with the wool and simmer together until the required depth of colour is reached. This will take about 30min, although weld will yield its colour very quickly.

Larch

Berries

Crush the berries with a large spoon or a potato masher and add to sufficient cold water to cover the wool. Bring to the boil, add the mordanted wool, turn down the heat and simmer together.

Bark and Pine Cones

Chop bark and break up pine cones and boil for 1–2hr. Add the wool and simmer together until the required depth of colour is reached.

Roots

Tie the roots in muslin and put wool and roots into cold water. Bring to the boil, then turn down the heat and simmer together until required colour is obtained.

Remove the pot from the heat and leave until cold. Take out the wool and rinse in several changes of water. Hang to dry. If dyeing with onion skins the smell will disappear if the wool is hung in the open air.

Lichens

The most important use of lichens to man is in the preparation of dyes. They are substantive dyes and need no mordants although with the addition of mordants it is possible to alter the colour and get a wider range of colours. Some lichens, including the Iceland moss (*Cetraria islandica*) have been used as food, but have little nutritional value. Reindeer moss – not a moss at all but a lichen, a species of *Cladonia* – is the food of deer in the Arctic regions.

Lichens are interesting plants made up of two organisms – an alga and a fungus. The alga contains chlorophyll and manufactures sugar to pass on to the fungus, which in turn protects the alga and passes nutrients to it. Lichens are found growing on rocks, roofs, walls, mile-stones, gravestones, trees and heathland. They absorb water and gasses through their upper surface and are very susceptible to pollution. If lichens are found growing anywhere in abundance it is a sign of a clean atmosphere. Stone fencing posts and old walls, especially of farm buildings, are good hunting grounds for lichen. It may sound obvious, but do not take lichen off gravestones, and it is polite to ask permission before creeping around strange farmyards with a knife and a paper bag. Lichens should be collected in winter or after heavy rain. It is important to realise that lichens are very slow-growing. A good-sized colony may take fifty years to develop. Never remove all the lichen from one place but leave enough for the plants to replenish themselves. There is an old saying in Poland about the picking of wild flowers – 'Always leave some for God.' This could equally well apply to the gathering of lichen.

There are three main types of lichens: crustaceous, foliose and fruticose. Crustaceous lichens are closely attached by the whole of the lower surface and not easily removed, particularly in dry weather, eg *Xanthoria parietina*. Foliose lichens are leaf-like, spreading horizontally over logs or the base of trees, eg *Lobaria pulmonaria*. The third type, fruticose lichens, are attached only at the base and may be found suspended from trees and gates, eg *Usnea cosmosa*.

Although lichens do not require a mordant it is possible to obtain different colours from the same lichen by using a mordant first. Put two test skeins – one mordanted with chrome and the other unmordanted – into a pot of *Xanthoria* and boil together. The unmordanted skein will be dyed pale cinnamon while the chrome mordanted skein will be pink. Crushed eggshells can be added either to the dye bath or to the mordant to provide further colours.

Dyeing with Lichens

Boil the wool and lichen together in a large pot by putting a layer of lichen in the bottom, then a layer of wool, then alternate layers of lichen and wool. About 1lb lichen to 1lb wool is the amount required although it is possible to use less lichen and thereby obtain a paler shade. Cover the wool and lichen with water and bring to the boil. Then turn down the heat and simmer until the required depth of colour is reached. This may take several hours. Take the pot off the heat and leave until cold. Rinse the wool several times until the water is clear. Shake the wool to remove the lichen. This will be a very fast dye.

Orchil Extraction

A preparation of lichen to produce beautiful red and purple shades is known as orchil. This method of making dye was first developed in Italy.

Use ½lb lichen to 1lb wool. Crumble the lichen well and put it into a container. Cover the lichen with 1 part of ammonium hydroxide to 1 part of water. Have enough of the solution to keep the lichen saturated. Cover the container to prevent fumes from escaping and keep in a warm place to work. The liquid, which is colourless to begin with, will gradually become dark red. Stir or shake the container daily. Leave for 6–28 days. After this, if you do not wish to use the solution, work powdered lime into it and roll it into small balls and keep for later use. In Scotland these balls are smoked and hung up until required; in this way they will keep indefinitely.

Orchil Dyeing

Orchil is not a very fast dye, so pre-mordant the wool with alum or tin. Do not use chrome, as this is an acid mordant, whereas the others are alkaline. Put the orchil solution into the dye pot. Add enough water to cover the wool. Enter wool to cold dye bath and heat to simmer as slowly as possible. When the dye bath has heated up, take it off the stove and let it stand for 1–3 days, according to the depth of colour required. Rinse the wool thoroughly in clear water. The dye bath can be re-used for lighter tones.

Dyeing in Winter

It is easier to obtain a large selection of dye plants during the summer months and some of these should be dried and stored for winter use. Weld, golden rod and chamomile should be cut when the plants first come into flower and hung to dry in the same way as other herbs. Do not use the plants after they have run to seed or the colour will be very poor. Pear leaves can be picked and put into fine mesh shopping bags or large squares of muslin and hung in the sun to dry. Bark, such as birch or plum bark, can be gathered at any time and pine cones are collected in the winter. Onion skins are obtainable most of the year and some evergreens, such as privet and holly leaves, can be used for dyeing. Roots are dug in autumn or winter, although it may not be very easy to locate some of the plants when the stems and flowers have died back into the rootstock, as with bedstraw, so it is advisable to dig them up at the end of July, dry them in the sun and store in bags or sacks. Lichens are obtainable at any time and easier to collect in winter. It is virtually impossible to scrape *Xanthoria* off a wall in the summer when there has been a prolonged dry spell.

List of Dye Plants

ANCHUSA (*Anchusa officinalis*) A red dye obtained from the roots of this plant has been used since Egyptian times. Use 1lb roots to 1lb wool previously mordanted with chrome.

APPLE Apple bark will give a dull yellow to gold depending on the length of time it is boiled. Use 1lb bark to 1lb wool previously mordanted with alum.

ASH (*Fraxinus excelsior*) The bark of this common tree will give varying shades of gold to wool mordanted with alum. Use 1lb bark to 1lb wool.

BEDSTRAW, HEDGE (*Galium mollugo*) Bedstraw is a close relation to the rose madder (*Rubia tinctoria*) which produces the colours turkey red, madder brown and madder yellow. Bedstraw is a pretty, wild plant with whorls of tiny white flowers appearing in cloud-like masses in early summer. It is one of the most useful natural dyes since it is one of the few which will produce red or pink. The roots are the part of the plant used – 1lb roots to 1lb wool. With an alum mordant the colour will vary from pale pink to apricot. Using a chrome mordant the roots of bedstraw will turn wool a deep red.

BEDSTRAW, LADY'S (*Galium verum*) Lady's bedstraw is very similar to hedge bedstraw and grows in the same places but it has bright yellow flowers. In Cheshire it was used to curdle milk for making the famous cheese and the flowers were said to give the cheese its distinctive flavour. In medieval times it was used to fill pallets, hence its name of lady's bedstraw. It is also known as wild rosemary, and cheese-rennet. The yellow flowers, if used with a chrome mordant, will give wool a yellow-gold colour.

BIRCH (*Betula pendula*) The birch is a graceful tree with silver bark and numerous small brown catkins in spring. Both the leaves and bark can be used as dyes. The leaves, using 1lb to 1lb wool mordanted with alum, will give a yellow dye. With a chrome mordant the colour will be a rich golden brown. The bark, if used with a chrome mordant, will give a pinkish brown. If an iron mordant is used with the bark, the colour will be a dull brown.

BLACKBERRY (*Rubus fruticosus*) The berries will give a lovely pinkish purple to wool previously mordanted with alum. Use 1lb berries to

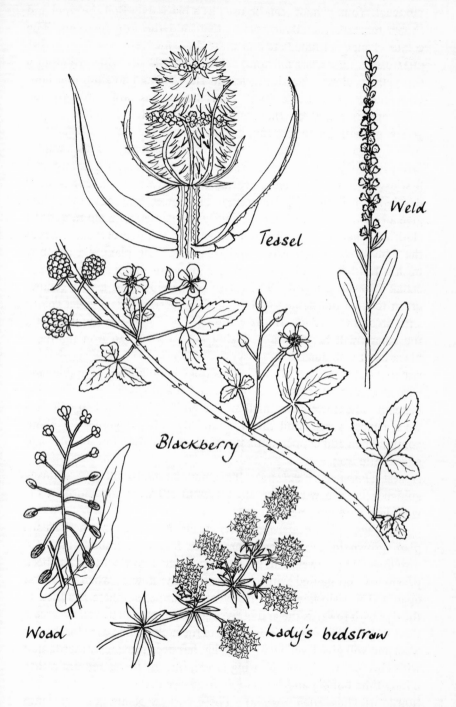

Teasel

Weld

Blackberry

Woad

Lady's bedstraw

1lb wool. Young shoots can be used as a black dye. Boil the wool and shoots together for about 30min, then add the iron mordant. The colour change is immediate and quite dramatic.

CHAMOMILE (*Anthemis tinctoria*)   The flower-heads will turn wool a soft yellow colour. Use 1lb flowers to 1lb wool and an alum mordant.

DOG LICHEN (*Peltigera canina*)   This lichen has large brown-green lobes and is found on the ground in woods. It dyes wool golden yellow or, with longer boiling, golden brown.

DYER'S GREENWEED; WOADWAX (*Genista tinctoria*)   This was a favourite plant of the dyers in the Middle Ages. Flemish immigrants first used it in the fourteenth century to obtain Kendal green, a colour developed in Kendal, Westmorland. The flowers and tops of the plant give a bright yellow to wool previously mordanted with alum, and the cloth will change to green when dipped in a solution of woad – hence the names dyer's greenweed and woadwax. The plant – a shrubby bush – has bright-yellow flowers and grows in rough grassy places.

ELDER (*Sambucus nigra*)   The leaves of the elder will give a yellow-green to wool mordanted with alum. The berries give a violet colour with an alum mordant. If 1oz common salt is added to the dye bath, the colour will be blue-grey. Using the bark and an iron mordant, black can be obtained.

FAT HEN (*Chenopodium album*)   This is a common plant of arable land with oval leaves that are grey-green above and silvery and glistening beneath. The flowers are small and green in spikes. Fat hen will turn wool a moss green. Boil the wool and dye plant together for about 30min. Then add copper sulphate mordant, boil for a few minutes and add a little iron.

FENNEL (*Foeniculum vulgare*)   This popular herb will give a lovely golden yellow to wool. Use 1lb leaves to 1lb wool and mordant the wool first with chrome.

GOLDEN ROD (*Solidago canadensis*)   This is a common herbaceous plant grown in gardens and sometimes found naturalised near old dwellings. The flowers will give a strong yellow to wool that has been previously mordanted with chrome. Pick the flowers when they first open and use 1lb flowers to 1lb wool. If copper sulphate is added to the dye bath towards the end of dyeing the colour will be yellow-green.

HOLLY (*Ilex aquifolium*)   The leaves of the holly can be used for dyeing wool and will give a yellow to wool that has been previously mordanted with chrome. It is a soft pleasing shade, but the leaves require rather a long time boiling and it is not an ideal dye plant.

HORSETAIL (*Equisetum arvense*)   These curious plants grow in damp places and are supposed to resemble prehistoric trees. Horsetails used with a chrome mordant will give a yellow-green to wool. Use 1lb of the plants to 1lb wool.

IRIS, PURPLE (Tall bearded) This is a rather surprising dye plant. The flowers of the ordinary purple iris, seen every June in cottage gardens, will give a lovely soft green to wool that has been previously mordanted with chrome. There is no need to pick all the new flowers off and spoil the plants, the old crumpled ones that need removing anyway will do just as well.

KNAPWEED (*Centaurea nigra*) The flower tops, using 1lb to 1lb wool and an alum mordant will give a pale yellow-green. Knapweed is a common wild plant of roadsides and waste places with purple thistle-like flowers, but the plant is not at all prickly. The dried seed-heads are attractive for winter decoration.

LARCH (*Larix decidua*) The larch is a beautiful tree, the only pine that is deciduous. The new leaves in spring are a lovely bright green, lighting up a wood like sunshine. If the needles are collected in autumn they will give a brown dye to wool that has been mordanted with alum.

LING (*Calluna vulgaris*) Use ling when it is in flower. The flowering tops will dye wool yellow-green if it has been mordanted first with alum.

MARIGOLD (*Calendula officinalis*) The flowers of the ordinary garden marigold will give a soft corn yellow to wool that has been mordanted with chrome.

OAK (*Quercus robur*) Use the bark of the oak tree, 1lb to 1lb wool boiling the bark first. Mordant the wool with alum. According to the time the wool and bark are boiled together the colour will vary from fawn to brown.

OAK LUNG; LUNGWORT; OAK RAG (*Lobaria pulmonaria*) A favourite with the medieval herbalists, this lichen is found on trees. It has large, green leaf-like lobes. It dyes wool orange.

ONION SKINS (*Allium cepa*) Use only the outer, brown papery skins to impart a deep cinnamon colour to wool previously mordanted with alum. After dyeing, hang the wool in the open air and the smell will disappear. If a chrome mordant is used the colour will be darker and richer.

PARMELIA SAXATALIS This is a common grey lichen growing on sundials, walls and trees in damp dark woods. It dyes wool golden brown.

PEAR (*Pyrus communis*) The leaves of the pear tree are used to give a rich gold to wool that has been mordanted with alum. Use 1lb leaves to 1lb wool. Pear leaves yield their colour quickly. They can even be used for dyeing when they are beginning to fall and have changed colour, although the colour will be weaker. Pear leaves give a good dye, fast to light and washing.

PHYSALIS; CHINESE LANTERNS (*Physalis franchetti*) This plant, grown for its orange seed-heads so popular in winter arrangements, is a good plant for dyeing. The leaves are the part used. Boil 1lb wool and 1lb leaves together for 30min. Then add copper-sulphate mordant to the dye bath. The colour will be a soft green. If an iron mordant is added as well as the copper sulphate the colour will be a moss green.

PINE CONES Pine cones will turn wool varying shades of brown, but need considerable boiling beforehand. With a chrome mordant the colour will be a pretty pinkish brown. If an iron mordant is added towards the end of dyeing the colour will be a good donkey brown.

PLUM Use plum bark for wool previously mordanted with alum, 1lb bark to 1lb wool. The colour will vary from fawn to golden brown depending on the length of time it is boiled. Plum bark is a good dye obtainable at any time of the year and one that yields its colour quickly and does not need endless boiling.

POPPY (*Papaver rhoeas*) The petals of the common corn poppy will give the most beautiful turquoise colour to wool mordanted with alum. Use 1lb petals for 1lb wool. This is only practical for small quantities of wool owing to the enormous amount of petals needed but would be lovely for a baby's jacket.

PRIVET (*Ligustrum vulgare*) The leaves of privet used with an alum mordant will give a yellow dye. The berries can also be used and yield a bluish-green dye.

RAGWORT; ST JAMES'S WORT (*Senecio jacobaea*) This plant, dedicated to St James, the patron saint of horses, is a common sight in meadows in autumn. The bright yellow flower-heads will give a yellow dye to wool that has been previously mordanted with alum.

RHODODENDRON The evergreen leaves of rhododendrons will give a brownish yellow to wool. Boil the wool and leaves together and then add an iron mordant to the dye bath.

ST JOHN'S WORT (*Hypericum pulchrum*) The flowering tops of the plant will give a yellow dye to wool that has been mordanted with alum. If a chrome mordant is used the colour will be a brownish green.

SEDGE (*Carex pendula*) This is a sedge of damp woods and shady places, its long drooping flowering spikes are unmistakable. Use these flowers for dyeing wool previously mordanted with alum. The colour will be a pretty pinkish gold.

TANSY (*Tanecetum vulgare*) The leaves of tansy, if picked in summer,

Field poppy

Anchusa

Tansy

Ragwort

Fennel

G

are very good for dyeing wool. Using an alum mordant and 1lb leaves to 1lb wool, the colour will be soft yellow. If a chrome mordant is used the colour will be brownish green. By using copper-sulphate mordant the colour from tansy leaves is a lovely soft green.

USNEA COSMOSA   The lichens belonging to the group known as *Usnea* are feathery, grey-green and seaweed-like, hanging in clumps from the trunks of trees. *Usnea* dyes wool yellow and, with prolonged boiling, brown. Copper sulphate added to the dye bath will produce a brownish green. *Usnea* is slow to yield its dye, requiring a longer time in the dye bath than some of the other lichens.

WALNUT (*Juglans regia*)   The shells and husks, if left to steep in cold water with the wool, will give a brown dye. No mordant is necessary as this is a substantive dye. The longer the wool is left to steep, the darker will be the colour. This dye should not be used for delicate wool as it makes the wool harsh.

WELD (*Reseda luteola*)   Weld was one of the three most important medieval dyes for wool – the other two being madder and woad – since it produces a very fast dye. It was also used with woad to produce green and is used in the preparation of a paint called Dutch pink. It grows 3–5ft high, with long dense racemes of small greenish yellow flowers. The leaves are long, glossy and undivided. Weld flowers from June to September. It can be used fresh or dried but it must be gathered before it has run to seed or the colour will be very poor. With an alum mordant the colour is bright yellow. If a chrome mordant is used it produces a lovely gold. If the mordant used is iron, the colour will be a deep brown.

WOAD (*Isatis tinctoria*)   Woad is a tall plant growing up to 3ft high. The lower leaves are oblong, while those on the stem are sessile and arrow-shaped. The tiny yellow flowers in panicles are succeeded by long, pendulous seed capsules, green at first, then turning brown when ripe. The plants are biennial, the seed being sown in April or May into the open ground to flower the following year.

This plant was used by the Ancient Britons for dyeing their clothes and staining their bodies. The leaves are the part of the plant used and produce a deep blue dye. It has long been cultivated in Lincolnshire and at the beginning of the century was grown there and used for dyeing policemen's uniforms.

To dye wool, first crush the leaves and then ferment them with lime. A green colour can be obtained by dyeing cloth first with weld and then with woad.

XANTHORIA PARIETINA   One of the commonest lichens and the best for dyeing purposes, *Xanthoria* forms bright orange patches on walls and roofs. Some lichens require prolonged boiling but *Xanthoria* yields its colour quickly and, with the use of mordants, it is easy to obtain about eight different colours with this lichen, from fawn to red and purple.

Some Tried and Recommended Dyes

Colour	Plant	Mordant
PINK	hedge bedstraw roots	alum
	hedge bedstraw roots	chrome
	lichen: *Xanthoria*	chrome
RED	hedge bedstraw roots	chrome
	lichen: *Xanthoria*	chrome
YELLOW	fennel leaves	chrome
	weld	alum
	chamomile	alum
	tansy leaves	alum
	lady's bedstraw flowers	chrome
	lichen: *Usnea*	—
GOLD	weld	chrome
	pear leaves	alum
	lichen: *Parmelia*	—
FAWN	oak bark	alum
	lichen: *Xanthoria*	—
	plum bark	alum
GINGER	birch leaves	chrome
	onion skins	alum
	lichen: *Usnea*	—
GREEN	horsetail	chrome
	iris flowers	chrome
	tansy	copper sulphate

	chinese lanterns	copper sulphate and iron
	lichen: *Usnea*	copper sulphate
	fat hen	copper sulphate and iron
PURPLE	blackberries	alum
	elderberries	alum
	lichen: *Xanthoria*	chrome and eggshells
BROWN	onion skins	chrome
	pine cones	chrome and iron
	weld	iron
BLACK	blackberry shoots	iron

NB Flowers as dye plants are only practical for small quantities of wool

7 Medicinal Herbs

The poppy-seeded draught which brings soft purple-
lidded sleep.

Oscar Wilde *Panthea*

Many of our present-day drugs are still obtained from plants, their uses developed from the old simples of our forefathers. There are many plants grown in the ordinary garden that yield drugs and the medicinal herbs make an interesting addition to a herb garden, but it should be stressed that no medicinal remedies should be tried except very simple ones, such as elderflower or chamomile tea for colds or depression, sage and ginger tea as a cure for colic, or external application of plants as a first-aid remedy for bites and stings. Medicinal herbs are grown primarily for their academic interest and never as a substitute for a doctor.

One of the favourite herbs of the monks was **belladonna** or deadly nightshade, a rare and beautiful wild plant that is still occasionally found growing by the ruins of old houses and abbeys. The whole plant is poisonous and is grown commercially for the drugs atropine and hyoscyamine which are obtained from the dried leaves.

Atropine is used to dilate the pupils of the eye and the name belladonna derives from the fact that Italian ladies of the fourteenth century used the juice of this plant to dilate their eyes and so make themselves appear more beautiful. The name atropa (*Atropa belladonna* is the Latin name) is from Atropos, one of the three Fates in classical history who cut the thread of Life. It was widely used in the Middle Ages as a narcotic. It was also known as 'dwale', and there is a reference to its use in Chaucer's 'Reeve's Tale', when the miller and his wife went to bed, they had drunk so much ale, 'hem needede no dwale'.

It is possible to purchase the seed, which will only germinate in a temperature of 55–60° F, but the plant should be treated with care. The berries are especially deadly and attractive to children and it is not a plant to be included in the average herb garden. The root can also be used and a liniment is made from it for the relief of neuralgia and rheumatism.

Henbane, a wild plant of the same family as belladonna, has similar narcotic properties and is cultivated for the drugs hyoscyamine and hyoscine, both sedative and hypnotic. Hyoscine is used in pills for travel sickness.

The **woody nightshade** (*Solanum dulcamara*) is a shrubby

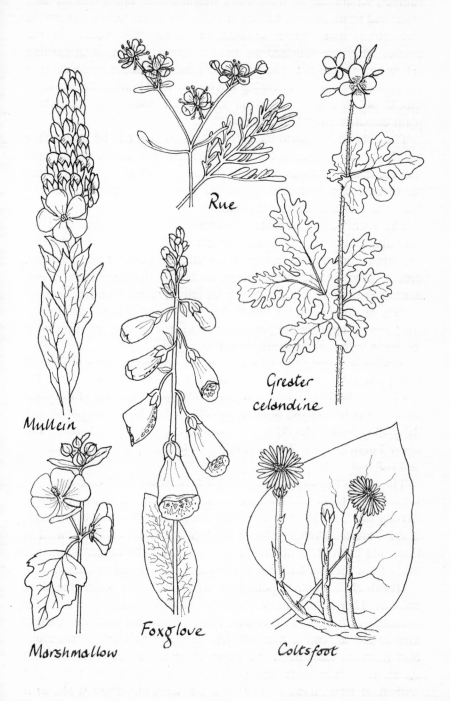

Rue

Mullein

Grester
celandine

Marshmallow

Foxglove

Coltsfoot

climber, scrambling up hedges to a height of 6ft. The leaves are dark green and heart-shaped, and the flowers, borne in clusters, are purple with conspicuous yellow anthers, resembling the flowers of the potato. They are followed by berries, green at first, then turning yellow and orange-red. The berries look most attractive in the autumn hedgerows among the changing leaves and blackberries, but children should be warned against them as they are poisonous. The whole plant contains narcotic properties.

The cultivated **potato** (*S. tuberosum*) is thought to be responsible for the disappearance of leprosy in Britain. It is interesting to note that the disease does not occur in those countries of the world where the potato is the staple diet. To soothe a burn, cut a potato in half and place the raw edge against the skin.

The roots of the **aconite** (*Aconitum napellus*) are also used for neuralgia and fevers. They are dug and dried in the autumn. Aconite has been known as a poison since ancient times. More recently, aconite was used to poison wells in North India in warfare, and applied to poison darts and spears for killing tigers. Its other name of Wolf's bane, refers to the fact that it was also used to poison wolves. All parts of the plant are poisonous so when handling the plant wear gloves in case the hands are scratched.

Arnica is a wild plant of woods and mountain pastures of Central Europe and the flowers and rhizomes are used to make a liniment for sprains and bruises and for treating chilblains. The leaves of the plant form a rosette and the flowers, growing 1–2ft high, are yellow and daisy-like. Arnica should not be used where the skin is broken, and never internally as it causes vomiting, giddiness, muscular weakness and collapse.

The **white bryony** is also used for bruises and in France the plant is known as 'herbe aux femmes battues' (plant of the beaten women). Bryony has a thick white rootstock resembling the root of the mandrake – hence its other name of English mandrake – and was used in many old cures. It contains the irritant poison, bryonine. A tincture made from the root has been used to allay coughing in pleurisy.

Hemlock is another poisonous wild plant that yields the drug coinine. This is an antidote to strychnine poisoning and used for treating hydrophobia and tetanus. Hemlock was known to the Ancient Greeks and the cup of hemlock that was given to Socrates was probably from the same plant that grows along the banks of streams and rivers. It reaches 6–8ft high with finely cut, chervil-like leaves and umbels of white flowers. The stem has dark blood-red spots, as if there as a warning, which makes it easy to distinguish from other umbelliferous plants. It sometimes accounts for the death of cattle. Hemlock is referred to in the Bible, where judgement is described as 'springing up as hemlock in the furrows of the field'.

Bear's foot hellebore (*Helleborus foetidus*), once used to cure cattle of pestilence, is also poisonous. The plant contains hellebrin and helleborin which have been used as a cardiac stimulant.

The best-known plant used for cardiac troubles is the **foxglove**. The use of digitalis from foxgloves was introduced into medicine by Sir William Withering in the eighteenth century. He discovered its properties after experimenting with a country remedy for dropsy using the plant. Foxgloves grow in open woods and on shady banks.

Agrimony was highly prized in medieval days for its medicinal properties. It was made into an ointment called arquebusade and used to heal the wounds of an arquebus – an old-fashioned handgun. An embrocation on sale in French chemists is known as 'eau d'arquebusade' and is thought to closely resemble this very old remedy. Agrimony, also known as church steeples, is a common wild plant of hedgerows and waysides with spikes of small yellow flowers and pinnate leaves. It was formerly thought to be effective in curing jaundice.

Many plants were used as a cure for pulmonary troubles: pulmonaria, lichen (*Lobaria pulmonaria*), mullein, alkanet, hyssop and coltsfoot among them. **Alkanet** (*Pulmonaria angustifolia*) is a spring-flowering plant with royal-blue flowers which are funnel shaped, and dark heart-shaped leaves which enlarge after flowering. The herb was dried and made into a tea, as were the bright blue flowers of **hyssop**. **Coltsfoot** flowers are the first to appear in the herb garden, opening early in February. The flowers are borne singly on soft stems covered with scales. They are a common sight in spring, covering waste ground and roadsides with patches of pale yellow. The heart-shaped leaves covered in woolly down appear after the flowers and the name of the plant comes from the shape of the leaves. Coltsfoot leaves boiled in milk are still used as a sure remedy for colds, coughs and bronchial troubles. Coltsfoot is also one of the main ingredients of herbal tobacco, being dried and used with other herbs such as betony. The plant spreads by underground rootstocks and needs to be kept in check.

Betony, a wild herb of waysides and woodlands, with red, purple-lipped flowers, was once highly esteemed as a cure for many ills and was grown in monastery gardens. The leaves can be dried and used as a tea for nervous headaches. An ointment was made with hog's grease and betony and used for burns and bruises.

Calamint, another wild herb, also known as wild basil, grows in grassy places and has pinky-mauve flowers in whorls round the stem and soft aromatic leaves. A tea was formerly made from the leaves and used for stomach ailments. Now, dried blackberry leaves are used as a treatment for dysentery.

Clary seeds, thought to promote lust, were also used for clearing the eyes, a seed being put into the corner of the eye to draw out foreign bodies. The name clary is from 'clear eye'.

Comfrey – the old 'knitbone' plant of the herbalists – was used for healing broken bones. The roots were ground up and made into a paste which was applied round the broken limb, the paste hardening as it dried and acting as a splint. A liquid extract of the root has been given internally as a treatment for gastric ulcers, and the dried root has been applied to wounds and ulcers as a decoction, or a poultice from the fresh root. The healing action of comfrey has been attributed to the presence of allantoin in the root. The common comfrey is *Symphitium officinale*. There is also the white-flowered form, tuberous comfrey, *S. tuberosum,* and the blue-flowered Russian comfrey, *S. peregrinum.* All have similar properties.

Many herbs, in particular those plants belonging to the mint family, have carminative properties – that is they soothe colic. Peppermint water is well known as an aid to digestion, and sage and ginger tea is a very simple and effective remedy for colic.

Sage and Ginger Tea

Put $\frac{1}{2}$tsp dried sage and $\frac{1}{2}$tsp ground ginger into a cup with 1tsp sugar. Fill with boiling water and cover with the saucer. Leave for 5min then strain and sip slowly.

Sage Syrup

Sage can also be used to make a soothing cough syrup.

Put 1 heaped tsp dried sage into a saucepan with 2 cups water. Bring to the boil, cover and simmer for 30min. Strain and add an equal quantity of vinegar and 1tbsp honey. Pour into a bottle and keep well corked. Take a teaspoonful when necessary.

Horehound is a hardy perennial with woolly stems, greyish leaves and small white flowers. It is occasionally found growing on cliff tops. The herb was used by monks for many ailments but especially for

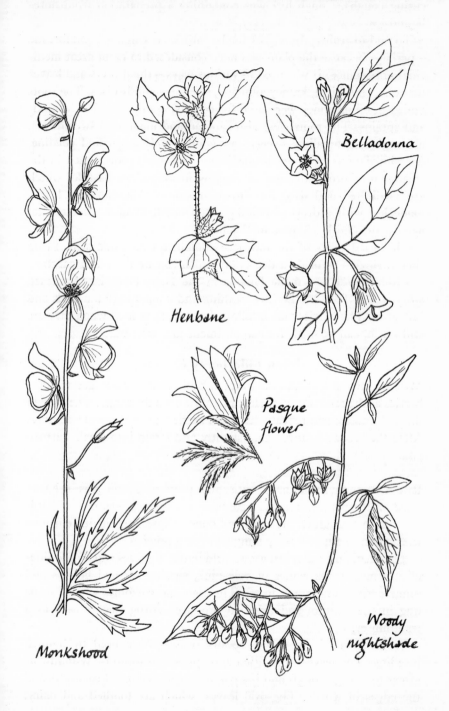

Henbane

Belladonna

Pasque flower

Monkshood

Woody nightshade

curing coughs. Cough lozenges containing a preparation from horehound leaves are still sold today.

To find **marshmallow** growing by the gate is a sign of good fortune – perhaps because the plant was once considered to be of great medicinal importance. It was used in various ways – the flowers and leaves for colic, childbirth, kidney ailments, swellings and bruises. The roots boiled in oil or honey were used for coughs, cramp, mastitis, wounds and sprains. The roots were also candied and made into sweetmeats, although marshmallow sweets now contain only sugar and gelatine. Marshmallow is still used in medicine. The dried root is used in the treatment of bronchitis and for making marshmallow pastilles which are medicated and used for throat infections. Marshmallow leaves made hot with a drop of boiling water and held in a handkerchief against the cheek will ease toothache.

The dried twigs of the **oak** tree contain quercitannic acid. From this astringent is made a decoction which can be used as a gargle.

Elderflower tea, made famous in the Hans Christian Andersen story 'Elder Tree Mother', is soothing and a good cure for colds and influenza. The berries which follow the flowers, if used when they are still green, can be made into an ointment to soothe burns.

Green Elderberry Cream

Melt 1lb lard in a dish in the oven, and add to it as many green elderberries as the fat will cover. Heat in a slow oven for 2–3hr. Then strain through muslin and repeat with more berries using the same mixture. After the second heating, cool slightly and strain into small warmed jars.

Rue was thought to have antiseptic properties and was used to ward off the plague. The herb contains a substance – rutin – which is thought to strengthen the teeth and bones. Squeezing the juice from a rue leaf on to a bee or wasp sting will bring relief.

The medicinal **valerian** grows wild in damp places and by the sides of streams. It has cymes of pale-pink, sweetly scented flowers and pinnate leaves and grows to 3ft. The plant has rhizomes which can be dug in the autumn and dried to produce a drug that is used as a tranquiliser.

Woundwort is so called because it was once used to staunch bleeding. The leaves were dried and applied to wounds. Woundwort grows to a height of 3ft and is a common wild plant of hedgerows and the edges of woods. The oval leaves, which are toothed and hairy, grow in pairs on opposite sides of the stem, while the crimson flowers, their lower lips spotted with white, grow in whorls around the stem.

Both **tansy** and **wormwood** have anthelmintic properties. Tansy tea was made and used for nervous disorders and fevers. Tansy wine was a popular remedy for worms and was used to procure abortions. Tansy cakes were also made and eaten after Lent to restore the body to good health after the restricted diet of the winter.

The lovely blue-flowered **flax** is grown commercially in large fields for the seeds which, when crushed, produce linseed. Linseed tea was a favourite drink prescribed for pregnant women to make childbirth easier. Linseed oil is obtainable from chemists and is good for bruises and sprains.

Thyme tea, made with fresh or dried leaves is supposed to be a good cure for sleeplessness and nightmares.

The seeds of the **spindle tree** were formerly powdered and used to destroy nits. The spindle is a shrub or small tree found in copses and hedgerows but it is less plentiful than it once was, as hedges are torn down to make larger fields or wider roads. The stems are green and the wood is smooth and hard and does not splinter. It was used for making spindles, hence its name, and gypsies made pegs and knitting-needles from the twigs. The grey-green oval leaves are in opposite pairs on the stems, and the small white flowers which open in May are followed by exquisitely beautiful fruits – orange capsules which split to reveal bright pink seeds.

All **poppies** are more or less narcotic. The opium poppy is well known as a drug source and yields laudanum. The scarlet flowers of the corn poppy – a familiar sight in late summer – were used in medieval times and made into a syrup to treat coughs and sore throats, and to induce sleep. When Anne Boleyn was about to be taken to the block to be beheaded, her ladies-in-waiting comforted her with a syrup made from poppies.

Wheat besides being grown for food was also prized for its medicinal properties. Oil pressed from wheat, if used warm, was supposed to heal ringworm; green corns if chewed healed the bites of mad dogs; and wheat flour mixed with egg yolk and honey was used to heal boils, ulcers and plague sores.

Saffron was highly valued in the sixteenth and seventeenth centuries as a drug herb. The saffron crocus (*Crocus sativus*) is often confused with the autumn crocus (*Colchicum autumnale*). Both have pale mauve flowers in August and September but the autumn crocus, or meadow saffron as it is sometimes called, has wide broad leaves while those of the true saffron are slender and grass-like. From the Middle Ages until the eighteenth century, saffron was cultivated on a large scale as it was thought to possess extraordinary medicinal powers and was used variously as a dye, flavouring, perfume or drug to shake off sleep and make a man merry. Only the stigmas of the plants were used to produce the dye or flavouring. More than 4,000 flowers were needed to yield 1oz saffron and so consequently it was very costly. The roots, if taken indiscriminately, are poisonous, but a very strong medicine was made from them by pounding the roots and making them into a syrup with honey and vinegar. A very small dose was taken at a time and was thought to cure pestilence, the pox, female disorders and hysteric depressions. An overdose produced immoderate convulsive laughter which sometimes ended in death. Saffron is mentioned in the Song of Solomon in the 'orchard of pomegranates and pleasant fruits; camphire with spikenard, and saffron'.

A herb pillow is considered to be very soothing and relaxing and can help to send one to sleep. It is also refreshing for anyone bedridden. It is easy to make since all it consists of is a large bag of muslin (or similar fine material) filled with dried herbs. The traditional herb pillow contains dried hops, but other herbs can be included, or the herbs used on their own. Any mixture of the following herbs would be suitable: marjoram, rosemary, lemon balm, mignonette, lavender, woodruff, bedstraw, chamomile, lime blossom, wild thyme and lad's love. Enclose the herb pillow in an ordinary pillow case which can be removed for washing, and place beneath the ordinary one.

In medieval times **lichens** were used in the treatment of disease. One of these, *Lobaria pulmonaria*, also known as lungwort, oak rag and oak lung, was used as a cure for pulmonary troubles. Culpeper recommended boiling it and making it into a syrup for coughs, shortness of breath and consumption, and for bathing ulcers. Usnic acid, found in *Usnea* and other lichens, has recently been found to have antibiotic properties and has been used to treat infections and wounds. Perhaps the use of lichens as a cure for all ailments, as they were used in medieval times, will be rediscovered.

Herbs were, and some still are, used to cure disease and ailments in animals. **Ragwort** was also known as St James's wort – St James was the patron saint of horses – and the plant was used for curing equine ailments. This striking plant that in summer covers pastures with sheets of gold is a great nuisance to farmers. It will quickly colonise neglected meadows and waste land and although sheep appear to eat the plant with impunity it is poisonous to cattle and donkeys. The

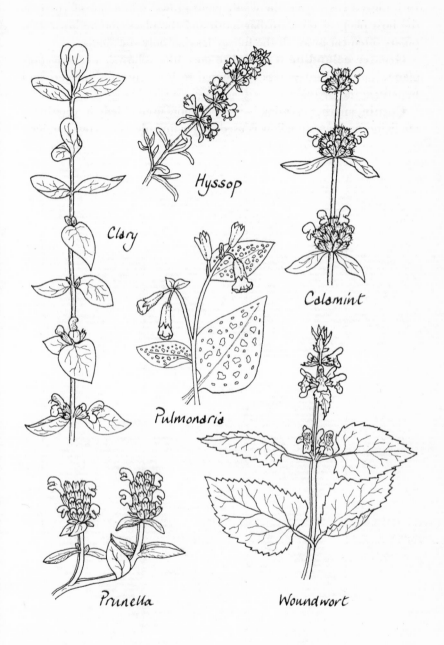

Clary

Hyssop

Calamint

Pulmonaria

Prunella

Woundwort

bright golden flowers are borne in corymbs, the leaves are toothed with ragged edges, and the whole plant grows to a height of 3ft. It is the host plant of the cinnabar moth and the black and yellow caterpillars often eat away all the foliage leaving only the stems.

Greater celandine was used to cure 'the yellows', a canine complaint, and **groundsel** was considered to be a cure for staggers and bot-worm in horses.

Cumin, another carminative herb, is now used chiefly in veterinary medicine, and marshmallow is used for healing ulcers on cows' udders.

8 Herbs as Cosmetics

She who on the first of May
Goes to the fields at break of day,
And washes in the dew from the hawthorn tree
Will ever after lovely be.

Old Nursery Rhyme

Herbs have been used as cosmetics for hundreds of years. The root of anchusa, a tall border plant with rough dark leaves and intensely blue flowers, produces a red dye which has been used for staining the lips and adding colour to the cheeks since Egyptian times. Italian ladies of the fourteenth century used to put belladonna juice in their eyes to enlarge the pupils and so make themselves appear more beautiful.

The traditional English way of achieving beauty was to wash in the dew on May Day. This was usually the dew from the hawthorn tree, but the dew drops that collect in the angles between the stem and leaves of teasels were thought to be specially magical and to make maidens fair.

Rain water is preferable to tap water for washing the face and hair as it is softer, and well water or spring water is even better. At one time every cottager used soapwort in place of soap for washing. Soapwort is a perennial plant which grows to a height of 3ft and, with its fragrant pale-pink flowers, resembles the garden sweet william. It grows wild in damp places and by river-banks. The leaves contain saponin and, when crushed, exude a liquid which produces a lather in water. It was cultivated near woollen mills for washing the newly woven cloth.

A good substitute for soap to wash greasy skin is oatmeal. Fill small muslin bags with fine oatmeal and use them with warm water for cleaning the face. Herbs such as rosemary, lavender and chamomile flowers will add a refreshing fragrance to a hot bath. Fill muslin bags with dried herbs and make a draw-string at the top of the bag. Hang the bag around the hot tap and let the water run through the herbs while filling the bath. After a tiring day sprigs of lavender added to the bath with 1tbsp salt are very reviving.

A mustard bath is a good old-fashioned remedy for tired and aching feet. Put 1tbsp mustard powder into a bowl of hot water and soak the feet.

Elderflowers and cowslip flowers will help to cure spots and blemishes. Put a handful of the blossoms – fresh or dried – in a cup and fill with boiling water. Leave to infuse for several hours, then bathe the face with the liquid.

A face pack can be made by mixing elderflowers or marigolds with honey. Spread on the face, leave for 5–10min, then wash off with cold water. Another way of making herbal face packs is to simmer herbs in a little water for 15min. Strain the herbs and spread them between pieces of muslin, apply the pack to the face and leave for 10min. Then wash the face with cold water. Herbs to use in this way include nettle tops, cowslip leaves, blackberry leaves and dandelion leaves.

An infusion of dill, lime blossom or nettle tops will strengthen and add lustre to your hair. Put a good handful of the herbs into a jug and add ½pt boiling water. Cover and leave for several hours. After washing your hair in the usual way, add the herbal infusion to the final rinsing water and rub well into the scalp.

To lighten your hair, fill a cup half full with dried chamomile flowers, and then fill up with boiling water. Cover and leave to stand for 1hr. Add this infusion of chamomile flowers to the final rinsing water, rubbing well into your hair. If you dry your hair in the sun the colour will be lighter still. Chamomile flowers give a lovely natural-looking golden light to brown hair. An infusion of fresh or dried rosemary leaves used in the same way will add lustre and depth to darker hair.

Mugwort is a common wild plant of waste land, belonging to the group of plants known as the artemesias. It was formerly used for all female ailments and for aiding childbirth, and was recommended by Culpeper as a remedy for taking too much opium. Mugwort is also known as midge plant, and an infusion of the leaves, sponged over the face and arms and left to dry will repel insects. Mugwort grows to 4ft high and has finely cut leaves which are bright green above and silvery grey beneath. The plant has dark red stems and small greyish flowers and in medieval times was thought to be a good blood purifier. Carvings in churches often depict mugwort leaves, perhaps because of the widespread belief in their value as healing plants, referred to in the old saying,

> If they would drink nettles in March
> And eat mugwort in May,
> So many young maidens
> Wouldn't go to the clay.

Chamomile flowers made into an infusion and used in the same way as mugwort, will also act as an insect-repellent.

Spinning is the age-old way of keeping hands smooth and soft, as fleece is very greasy and rich in natural lanolin. To whiten hands rub

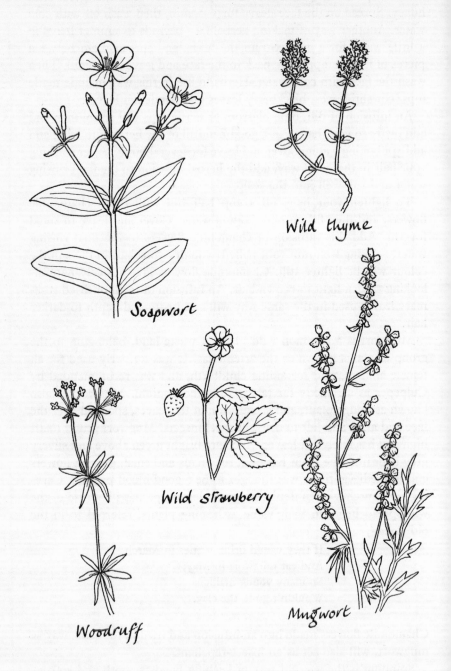

Soapwort

Wild thyme

Wild strawberry

Woodruff

Mugwort

them with a cut slice of cucumber or lemon. Rubbing hands with dry mustard powder after slicing onions will help to remove the smell.

Dandelions and celandine are used in the country to remove warts and corns. Both plants have juice in their stems. The juice of the dandelion stains the hands brown and if squeezed on to warts will make them disappear. The celandine to use is the greater celandine – at one time used for eye troubles and jaundice. The plant grows 2–3ft high with greyish leaves which are lobed, and yellow four-petalled flowers. It is found growing as a wild plant on waste ground and walls, usually in the vicinity of old buildings. The stems contain acrid juice which can be squeezed on to warts and corns to make them disappear, and the whole plant is somewhat poisonous.

To whiten teeth, rub them over with a fresh sage leaf and eat plenty of strawberries; strawberries whiten the teeth as they contain acid.

If you feel that you have a problem with being overweight, chewing an elm leaf is supposed to take away hunger. It is said that many a ploughman chewed on elm leaves while awaiting his lunch.

Finally, good health is the best aid to beauty. Eat plenty of fresh green vegetables and fruit and always use honey in place of sugar whenever possible.

Appendix: Table of Flowering

Common name	Latin name	Flowering time	Height	Part used
aconite	*Aconitum napellus*	June–Aug	3–4ft	roots
agrimony	*Agrimonia eupatoria*	June–Sept	2ft	flowers, leaves
alchemilla	*Alchemilla vulgaris*	June–Aug	12–18in	leaves
alkanet	*Pulmonaria angustifolia*	February	12in	leaves
anaphalis	*Anaphalis nubigena*	Aug–Sept	12in	flowers
anchusa	*Anchusa officinalis*	May–June	4–5ft	flowers, root
angelica	*Angelica archangelica*	May	4–5ft	stems
arnica	*Arnica montana*	May–July	1–2ft	flowers, root
ash	*Fraxinus excelsior*	March	80–100ft	wood, fruit
balm, lemon	*Melissa officinalis*	June–July	3ft	leaves
basil	*Ocimum basilicum*	September	12in	leaves
bay	*Laurus nobilis*	April–May	12–15ft	leaves
bedstraw	*Galium verum*	June	18in	flowers, roots
beech	*Fagus sylvatica*	April–May	100ft	leaves, wood
belladonna	*Atropa belladonna*	June–Aug	4–5ft	leaves, root
bergamot	*Monarda didyma*	July–Aug	2–4ft	flowers, leaves
betony	*Stachys betonica*	June–Aug	18in	leaves
blackberry	*Rubus fruticosus*	June–Sept	climbing	leaves, fruit
blackcurrant	*Ribes nigrum*	May	3–4ft	fruit
borage	*Borago officinalis*	May–July	2ft	flowers, leaves
brooklime	*Veronica beccabunga*	May–July	9in	leaves
broom	*Cytisus scoparius*	May	4–5ft	flowers, stems
bryony, white	*Bryonia dioica*	June–July	climbing	root
burnet, salad	*Poterium sanguisorba*	June–Aug	12–18in	leaves
calamint	*Clinopodium vulgare*	July–Sept	1–3ft	leaves
caraway	*Carum carvi*	May	2ft	seeds
carline thistle	*Carlina vulgaris*	July–Sept	1–2ft	flowers
catmint	*Nepeta cataria*	June	9–12in	leaves
celandine, greater	*Chelodonium major*	May–Sept	2–3ft	stem, leaves
celandine, lesser	*Ranunculus ficaria*	Feb–April	6in	leaves
chamomile	*Anthemis nobilis* *Anthemis tinctoria*	June–Sept	9in	flowers
chervil	*Anthriscus cerefolium*	April–May	1ft	leaves
chicory	*Cichorium intybus*	July–Sept	2–5ft	leaves, roots
chinese lanterns	*Physalis franchetti*	June–Aug	2–3ft	leaves, fruit
chives	*Allium schoenoprasum*	July	9in	leaves
clary	*Salvia horminum*	July–Sept	12–18in	seeds
coltsfoot	*Tussilago farfara*	February	9in	leaves

Common name	Latin name	Flowering time	Height	Part used
comfrey	*Symphytum officinalis*	May–July	3–4ft	leaves, root
coriander	*Coriandrum sativum*	July–Aug	12–18in	seeds
cowslip	*Primula veris*	April–May	12in	flowers
cuckoo pint	*Arum maculatum*	April	12in	roots
cumin	*Cuminum cyminum*	July–Aug	12–18in	seeds
daisy	*Bellis perennis*	March–Oct	6in	leaves
dandelion	*Taraxacum officinale*	May–Sept	12in	all parts
datura	*Datura sauveolens*	July–Sept	10–12ft	leaves
dill	*Anethum graveolens*	September	3–4ft	leaves, seeds
dog rose	*Rosa canina*	June–Sept	climbing	flowers, fruit
dog's mercury	*Mercurialis perennis*	February	9in	flowering shoot
dogwood	*Thelycrania sanguinea*	June	6–8ft	stems
elder	*Sambucus nigra*	June	20ft	all parts
elm	*Ulmus procera*	March	100ft	leaves, wood
eryngo	*Eryngium maritimum*	July–Aug	2ft	roots
fennel	*Foeniculum vulgare*	Aug–Sept	2ft	leaves
feverfew	*Chrysanthemum parthenium*	June–Sept	18–24in	flowers, leaves
flax	*Linum usitatissimum*	July	18in	stems, seeds
foxglove	*Digitalis purpurea*	June–July	3–5ft	leaves
goosegrass	*Galium aparine*	June–Sept	2–4ft	leaves
groundsel	*Senecio vulgaris*	Jan–Dec	9in	leaves, shoots
hawthorn	*Crataegus monogyna*	May	20–30ft	leaves, berries
heart's ease	*Viola arvensis*	May–Sept	9in	leaves, flowers
helichrysum	*Helichrysum monstrosum*	July–Sept	2ft	flowers
hellebore (bear's foot)	*Helleborus foetidus*	Feb–May	18in	root
hemlock	*Conium maculatum*	June–July	6–7ft	leaves
henbane	*Hyoscyamus niger*	June–Aug	1½–2ft	leaves
honesty	*Lunaria biennis*	April–May	2–3ft	seed-heads
horehound	*Marrubium vulgare*	July–Oct	1–1½ft	leaves
horseradish	*Armoracia rusticana*	July	3ft	roots
hyssop	*Hyssopus officinalis*	June–July	15in	flowers, leaves
lad's love	*Artemesia abrotanum*	September	2ft	leaves
lavender	*Lavendula officinalis*	June–July	1½–3ft	flowers, leaves
lily, Madonna	*Lilium candidum*	June–July	3–4ft	flowers
lime	*Tilia europaea*	July	100ft	flowers, wood
lovage	*Ligusticum levisticum*	July–Aug	4ft	leaves
mandrake	*Atropa mandragora*	July	12in	root

Common name	Latin name	Flowering time	Height	Part used
marigold	*Calendula officinalis*	April–Oct	15in	flowers
marjoram	*Origanum vulgare*	June–July	18in	leaves
marshmallow	*Althea officinalis*	July–Aug	2–3ft	all parts
meadowsweet	*Filipendula ulmaria*	June–Aug	2–3ft	roots
mint:				
bowles	*Mentha rotundifolia*	Aug–Sept	2ft	leaves
eau-de-Cologne	*M. citrata*	Aug–Sept	2ft	leaves
pennyroyal	*M. pulegium*	September	6in	leaves
peppermint	*M. piperita*	July–Sept	2ft	leaves
Spanish	*M. requienii*	July–Sept	1in	leaves
spear	*M. spicata*	July–Sept	18in	leaves
moneywort	*Lysimachia nummularia*	June–Sept	creeping	leaves
mugwort	*Artemesia vulgaris*	July–Aug	3–4ft	leaves
mullein	*Verbascum thapsus*	June–July	4–6ft	leaves, stem
mustard, brown	*Brassica juncea*	June	2½ft	seeds
mustard, white	*Sinapis alba*	June	2–2½ft	seeds
myrtle	*Myrtus communis*	June	12ft	flowers, leaves
nasturtium	*Tropaeolum majus*	July–Oct	climbing	all parts
nettle	*Urtica dioica*	July	3–5ft	green tops, seeds
nicandra	*Nicandra physaloides*	July–Aug	3–5ft	leaves, seeds
nightshade, black	*Solanum nigrum*	July–Sept	1–2ft	
nightshade, woody	*Solanum dulcamara*	July–Sept	climbing	
oak	*Quercus robur*	May	100ft	fruit, wood
orris	*Iris florentina*	May–June	2ft	root
parsley	*Petroselinum crispum*	August	3ft	leaves
pasque flower	*Pulsatilla vulgaris*	April	9in	leaves
periwinkle	*Vinca major*	March–May	trailing	leaves, stems
poppy	*Papaver rhoeas*	June–Sept	2ft	flowers, seeds
potato	*Solanum tuberosum*	June	2–3ft	root tubers
prunella	*Prunella vulgaris*	June–Sept	9in	leaves
pulmonaria	*Pulmonaria officinalis*	Feb–March	9in	leaves
pumpkin	*Cucurbita pepo*	July–Aug	trailing	fruit
purslane	*Portulaca oleracea*	September	6in	leaves, stem
ragwort	*Senecio jacobaea*	July–Sept	2–3ft	leaves, flowers
rhodanthe	*Helipterum manglesii*	July	1–1½ft	flowers
rocket	*Eruca sativa*	August	9in	leaves, stem
rosemary	*Rosmarinus officinalis*	April	5–6ft	flowers, leaves
rue	*Ruta graveolens*	May–Aug	2–3ft	leaves
saffron	*Crocus sativus*	Aug–Sept	6in	flowers, root
sage	*Salvia officinalis*	July–Sept	2–3ft	leaves

Common name	Latin name	Flowering time	Height	Part used
sainfoin	*Onobrychis viciifolia*	June–July	18in	whole plant
santolina	*Santolina chamaecyparissus*	August	3–4ft	leaves
savory, summer	*Satureja hortensis*	July–Aug	15in	leaves
savory, winter	*Satureja montana*	July–Aug	15–18in	leaves
scarlet pimpernel	*Anagallis arvensis*	June–Sept	6in	leaves
soapwort	*Saponaria officinalis*	June	3ft	leaves
sorrel	*Rumex acetosa*	June	2–3ft	leaves
spindle	*Euonymus europaeus*	May	12ft	seeds, wood
statice	*Statice sinuata*	July–Sept	2ft	flowers
sunflower	*Helianthus annuus*	Aug–Oct	6–8ft	flower buds, seeds
sweet Cicely	*Myrrhis odorata*	May–June	2–3ft	leaves, root
sweet flag	*Acorus calamus*	June–July	4ft	leaves
tansy	*Tanacetum vulgare*	July–Aug	2–3ft	flowers, leaves
tarragon, French	*Artemesia dracunculus*	July	2–3ft	leaves
tarragon, Russian	*Artemesia dracunculoides*	July	4–5ft	leaves
teasel	*Dipsacus fullonum*	July	4–6ft	flower-heads
thyme, garden	*Thymus vulgaris*	June–July	12in	leaves
thyme, wild	*Thymus serpyllum*	July–Sept	trailing	leaves
valerian	*Valeriana officinalis*	June–Aug	3ft	roots
violet, sweet	*Viola odorata*	March–April	6in	flowers, leaves
wallflower	*Cheiranthus cheiri*	April–June	1–2ft	flowers
walnut	*Juglans regia*	May	40–100ft	fruit, wood
watercress	*Nasturtium officinale*	May–Oct	12–18in	leaves, stem
weld	*Reseda luteola*	June–Aug	3–5ft	flowering tops
wheat	*Triticum aestivum*	June	2ft	whole plant
wild chervil	*Anthriscus sylvestris*	May	3ft	leaves
wild strawberry	*Fragaria vesca*	April–July	9in	fruit
woad	*Isatis tinctoria*	May	2–3ft	leaves
wood anemone	*Anemone nemorosa*	April	9in	leaves
woodruff	*Asperula odorata*	May–June	12in	whole plant
wormwood	*Artemesia absinthium*	July–Sept	3–5ft	leaves, flowers
woundwort	*Stachys sylvatica*	June–Sept	2–3ft	leaves
xeranthemum	*Xeranthemum annuum*	July	1½–2ft	flowers
yarrow	*Achillea millefolium*	June–Sept	1½–2ft	leaves
yew	*Taxus baccata*	Feb–March	20–50ft	wood

Bibliography

Barton, J. G. *Wild Flowers* (Spring Books, 1963)

Beedell, Suzanne. *Wine Making and Home Brewing* (Sphere, 1969)

Brightman, F. H. *The Oxford Book of Flowerless Plants* (Oxford, 1966)

Brownlow, Margaret. *Herbs and the Fragrant Garden* (Darton, Longman and Todd, 1963)

Culpeper, Nicholas. *Complete Herbal* (first published 1652; Foulsham, 1973)

Grigson, Geoffrey. *A Herbal of all Sorts* (Phoenix House, 1959)

Hibberd, Shirley. *Familiar Garden Flowers* (Cassell, Peter, Galpin, 1880)

Lloyd, H. S. *The Popular Cocker Spaniel* (Popular Dog Publishing Co, 1933)

Mabey, Richard. *Food For Free* (Collins, 1972)

Martin, W. Keble. *The Concise British Flora in Colour* (Ebury Press, Michael Joseph, 1965)

Rohde, Eleanour Sinclair. *The Old English Herbals* (Longmans, 1972)

Scott, T. H. and Stokoe, W. J. *Wild Flowers of the Wayside and Woodland* (Warne, 1955)

Thurstan, Violetta. *The Use of Vegetable Dyes* (Dryad Press, 1972)

Warren, C. Henry. *Essex* (Robert Hale, 1950)

White, Gilbert. *The Natural History of Selborne and the Naturalist's Calendar* (first published in 1789; Crescent Press, 1974)

Young, Andrew. *A Prospect of Flowers* (Jonathan Cape, 1945)

Acknowledgements

I would like to thank my family for all their help and encouragement. The book has been an excuse for many household duties being left undone, and my two children have always been willing to lend a helping hand, as has my husband, who took the photographs. I would also like to thank all my friends who have given me plants and cuttings for my herb garden, especially Pamela Twinn, whose herb garden is shown in plate 2.

I am grateful to Mr R. H. Butcher of Reckitt and Colman, Norwich, for much helpful information concerning mustard, and to Mrs R. Martin for her country wine recipes.

I would like to thank Hugh Johnson for his advice and kindness in reading the manuscript.

Index